Silent No More

PRAISE FOR *SILENT NO MORE*

"My people matter." It is a message that every individual needs to hear. In a world that is so accessible and yet so broken, this book gives both a timely and timeless message. While some authors only use their words, Jody includes her heart. We get an authentic encounter to the realities of life, but also witness the power of God. It is in this space that Jody masterfully and graciously reminds us of who and what we are called and created to be. Her willingness to answer this call will inspire generations to come to be *Silent No More.*

-Dr. Jevon Caldwell-Gross, pastor of Teaching & Guest Experience, St. Luke's United Methodist Church

Having the privilege of watching Jody grow and flourish in her Christian walk over the years has been a special joy! Jody has overcome adversity—professional and personal obstacles in her path—with the grace that comes from a strong and resilient faith. In sharing her journey, she will touch and inspire every reader. Leader, teacher, servant and so much more—Jody is a blessing to know, love and call friend.

-Nancy Frick, MDiv, Community Spiritual Director, Indianapolis Great Banquet

When meeting Jody Dedon years ago, within seconds, I knew she was a woman of extreme kindness and powerful optimism. Since that time, I have witnessed her positivity energize those around her in good times and strengthen them during the bad. While Jody and I often have different perspectives, *Silent No More* is an important read for anyone looking to learn from and be inspired by an earnest, resilient leader grounded in her faith.

-**Christina Hale,** author, speaker, and strategist

When we read the Bible, our hearts are inspired by a God who is actively speaking and moving in the lives of people. Yet, when we look at our own lives, we struggle to hear God's voice. Jody L. Dedon's *Silent No More* is a salient reminder that God is still speaking and seeking us today. Her journey will empower you to acknowledge your own God-given worth and equip you with ways to hear God's voice through the noise of toxic work environments, divorce, and grief. Lift your voice, grow your faith and breakthrough to God's expansive vision for your life as you read her words of wisdom and hope.

-**Rev. Nicole Caldwell-Gross,** pastor of
Mobilization & Outreach,
St. Luke's United Methodist Church

Countless voices urge us to be more engaged. Countless concerns demand greater attention. While living a full life of abundant service, Jody Dedon came to find, inside herself, the singular expression of God's love—her own voice. *Silent No More* takes us along on her very personal journey and helps us discover a path of recovery and healing from our own overprogrammed and burdened existence. What is our Creator's wish for us and why is it so often buried in a hoard of assumed obligations and external expectations? Ultimately, it was in confronting her tremendous challenges that Jody returned to where she'd begun, in understanding and embrace of God's love and commandment for each of us. The fog of toxic relationships and deep personal loss is lifted through insightful questions and thoughtful response revealing a course for us all. If God believes that we matter, why don't we believe it?

-Terry W. Anker, The Anker Consulting Group

I first met Jody when I interviewed her to be a director for a large not-for-profit. I was struck by her personal story that revealed her passion and resilience. With Jody, I knew I would be hiring someone with strong character. She has a way of tackling challenges that come her way with positivity and confidence, no matter what her circumstances might be. Jody showed me that when life knocks you down, you get back up—

not because you need to be tough, but because she knows that God is always there to pick you up and dust you off. Even during the storms of life, she embraces the moment she is in and keeps her eyes and heart open to what God has in mind for her. Jody's example of how she lives life is a radiant beacon for others to see and follow.

-Daniel Folta, managing consultant,
American Philanthropic

SILENT NO MORE

Finding Your Worth Through God's Eyes

JODY L. DEDON

NEW YORK

LONDON • NASHVILLE • MELBOURNE • VANCOUVER

Silent No More

Finding Your Worth Through God's Eyes

© 2023 Jody L. Dedon

Published in New York, New York, by Morgan James Publishing. Morgan James is a trademark of Morgan James, LLC. www.MorganJamesPublishing.com

Proudly distributed by Ingram Publisher Services.

Unless otherwise marked, Scriptures taken from THE HOLY BIBLE, NEW INTERNATIONAL VERSION (NIV)®. Copyright© 1973, 1978, 1984, 2011 by Biblica, Inc.™. Used by permission of Zondervan.
Scriptures marked KJV are taken from the KING JAMES VERSION, public domain.
Scriptures marked ESV are taken from THE HOLY BIBLE, ENGLISH STANDARD VERSION® Copyright© 2001 by Crossway, a publishing ministry of Good News Publishers. Used by permission.
Scriptures marked NKJV are taken from the NEW KING JAMES VERSION®. Copyright© 1982 by Thomas Nelson, Inc. Used by permission. All rights reserved.

Morgan James BOGO™

A **FREE** ebook edition is available for you or a friend with the purchase of this print book.

CLEARLY SIGN YOUR NAME ABOVE

Instructions to claim your free ebook edition:
1. Visit MorganJamesBOGO.com
2. Sign your name CLEARLY in the space above
3. Complete the form and submit a photo of this entire page
4. You or your friend can download the ebook to your preferred device

ISBN 9781631959134 paperback
ISBN 9781631959141 ebook
Library of Congress Control Number:
2022933579

Cover & Interior Design by:
Christopher Kirk
www.GFSstudio.com

Morgan James is a proud partner of Habitat for Humanity Peninsula and Greater Williamsburg. Partners in building since 2006.

Get involved today! Visit MorganJamesPublishing.com/giving-back

FOR HIS GLORY
and dedicated to all the angels in my life

TABLE OF CONTENTS

ACKNOWLEDGMENTS

My mom, who was my champion and greatest fan, knew I had finally listened to God's calling and was thrilled and excited to read this book. While she never got to hold it in her hands or read a single word, Mom, your heart beats with mine as I wrote each word. I love you forever!

To my husband Craig—and my very best friend—for believing in me always and for giving me exactly what I've always searched for and needed: unconditional love and acceptance to be *me*. I love you, L. DWPs forever.

Graham, you have always been my greatest gift from God. You've been by my side through it all. My greatest blessing. I couldn't have asked for a better son. I am so proud of you.

Brayden, an angel that continues to inspire me every day to share His truth to the world that everyone is valuable and deeply cherished. I love you, sweetheart, and miss you every day.

Jack, your love and acceptance of others inspires me every day. Keep bringing you. The world needs more Jacks.

Carter, I am more proud of you than you'll ever know. Thanks for always making me laugh and bringing your spirit. Continue to be great and believe in yourself. You are that awesome.

Theresa, Yvonne, Jonna, Mike, John, and Amy: my network of friends who have pushed me along, believed in me, and stood for me along the way . . . I believe in you too. Go live your dreams. The view on the top of the mountain is breathtaking.

And Morgan James Publishing, thank you for believing in my message.

FOREWORD

A s a pastor of a large congregation, I am humbled by how little I know about the people I speak to each week. I can see faces every Sunday but not know much beyond the names of many—perhaps what they do for a living and maybe a little about their families. Oftentimes, it takes experiences that connect me in a pastoral way before I get a glimpse into the souls of church people, and usually, these experiences are painful ones. Such is the case with Jody Dedon.

Learning about the death of their adult son several years ago, I got to sit with Jody and her husband, Craig, one afternoon in their living room. I could quickly tell these are people of deep faith and trust in God. Without hiding their grief or downplaying their pain, they exemplified a closeness to God I recognized as something that had been grown over a lifetime. Like a deep well from which you can draw fresh water, they had a connection to God that gave them peace even during anguish and sorrow.

When Jody shared with me that she was writing a book about her relationship with God and the difference it makes in her life, I was grateful. Jody has a story to share. Her story is relatable to just about anyone. If you've gone through a loss that makes you second guess yourself or leaves you feeling as if your life has been erased, you need to read this book. If you believe in God, but it has been a long time since you've felt God's presence—so long that you are starting to question if you have any faith at all—you need to read this book. If religious activities bring little joy and cause you to ask, "Why bother?" then you need to read this book. If your love and passion and excitement for living all feel as though they are evaporating, you must read this book.

But *Silent No More* is not just a book. It is a virtual reality. You will get more than a glimpse into Jody's soul. She will invite you into her life and share her experiences, all of which lead to her most important experience: God. You may well have your own God-encounters as you read these pages.

At times, you will feel as if you're learning from a great mystic and spiritual mentor. At other times, you will feel as if you're having coffee with someone who is becoming an important friend. At still other times, you will hear your own questions about life and faith being expressed. A book that does these things becomes a valuable resource, not just because we learn about the author, but because we learn about ourselves. Jody's story will cause us to think about our own story, what is being told, and what we want to tell.

Jody has a story to share and so do you. All of our stories start and end with God. Life and faith are what happen between our beginnings and endings regardless of whether or not we are persons of faith. More important than what we believe about God is the knowledge that God believes in us.

Jody will help you believe. I know that because she helps me believe. When I experience such faith in a person who listens to me preach every Sunday, it helps me believe that what I say are not just words. I am offering a bridge to the One who gives us purpose, value, and hope. This book is just such a bridge. I hope you enjoy it as Jody walks with you across it, and may this book help you consider the other bridges God can build through your life.

Being Jody's pastor is an incredible honor. When I am in her company, I realize I am with someone who knows God in a real, life-changing way. Her faith rubs off on you. This book will put you in Jody's company and help you not just believe in God but know Him too.

—**Reverend Rob Fuquay,** senior pastor at St. Luke's United Methodist Church and author

INTRODUCTION

"Let my people go, that they may serve me."
Exodus 8:1

Moses was instructed by God to go to Pharaoh and declare these words: "Let my people go, that they may serve me." This was the single point in history that drove needed change to end the slavery of the Israelites. This phrase allowed nations to flourish and rewrote the path of history.

Breathe that in for a moment. Defining moments such as these are life changers. Defining moments sometimes take years to come to fruition; other times, they happen in an instant. Defining moments change the course of our lives forever.

This journey started at such a point—a crossroads really. A decision to stay and remain tortured by the toxic environment I was enduring or to simply leave and walk away. Then God spoke. He had a message for me that would redefine who I am and my life going forward.

My people matter.

As a confessed endless workaholic, a deep-diver into organizational problems and issues, I've spent most of my life heads-down in work. Working endlessly toward solutions bringing change and acclaim to my employers' missions. I ride the conveyer belt of continuous improvement, with an occasional glance up at times but only to return to the deep dive of work the very next moment. I am a lover of *doing*. Much like a golden retriever addicted to the pats of praise sought by doers like me. So when I heard His voice, it stopped me in my tracks.

My people matter.

In the still silence, He finally had my attention. It saddens me to think of the years that He had been waiting for me to notice. To finally be still enough to hear his voice. How long had He been speaking? Had He been giving me insights along the way? How many had I missed while working . . . working . . . doing . . .

We are our best selves when we dare to stand bare before Him, asking, seeking, and knocking.

"My people matter" were the words God spoke, and it was past time for me to take notice. Past time for me to stop my hurried, frantic pace and finally calm myself enough to hear His quiet voice. Past time for me to listen and obey and finally hear His purpose for my life and to devote my life to Him, making time for His people. After all, this was what He had designed me to do. To speak the truth and empower them. To lift them up and tell the news that He wanted to be told.

Whether you believe in being God-inspired or not, from when I was a very young child, I heard Him calling me. I have heard His voice throughout my life—sometimes even when I didn't want to hear it, but when I wanted to do life my own way instead. I was born for this moment. Every caption of my life has led to this defining moment. To finally put into words the message that I've heard.

I am thankful for the defining moments that led to this day, for the chapters of my life that defined who I am. Especially, for the treatment that was so undeserved, stacked with unconscionable hatred and disrespect, which led me to this single moment in life. A defining moment so powerful that it unleashed the *truth*. A truth so powerful that has been waiting to be set free.

My people matter.

Bondage no more. I hope that through this book, you will be *set free*. My wish is that every chain will be broken—each one that keeps you from living and being who He made you to be.

Today, my chains are gone. I am *SILENT NO MORE.*

Chapter 1

LESS THAN

Titles. They define our reality. The first question we ask upon meeting one another is, "What's your name?" followed by "What do you do?" In an instant, we seem to define our importance with our responses. If you say, "I'm the CEO" or "president," the thoughts that can follow include, "You're important. You're smart. You're accomplished. You're *valued*." On the other hand, if you say, "I recently resigned" or "I just started my new business," doubt settles in and is usually followed by a host of questions to discern your importance.

We make our initial assessment about a person's worth in a split second without evaluating things like character, qualities, values, or beliefs.

After recently resigning from a position, I experienced this very situation. As I went from executive director of a significant nonprofit organization to an entrepreneur in a day, my friends asked, "What happened? Was there a problem? What is the "real reason?"

It didn't feel good. When did we begin defining ourselves by the titles we possess? After all, I was still the same person. I thought the same. I still had the same work history that I had earned throughout my career. I still had the same work ethic. Yet this time, perceptions were different.

When I had first landed "the job," friends commented on how quickly I had risen through the ranks, how influential this position was. Suddenly, I was "someone." I was sought-after by leaders throughout the community. Everyone wanted to celebrate, and people were clamoring to get on my schedule. Yet, after I resigned . . . in a single moment, I had become "less than." I was just another person, and people seemed to now look away.

This curious phenomenon led me on a journey of rediscovering "value." I was at the crossroads of discovery. Throughout this adventure, I learned vital truths and examined life messages that we all need to explore and contemplate. It has been a journey that has redefined my existence, brought clarity and purpose, and propelled me to step into my future—a future that awaits us all.

It's a journey that I hope you'll take with me. A journey to be set free and be *Silent No More*.

STEP ONE: DEFINE YOUR EXISTENCE

We are our true selves when we are unabashed and bare. When we come before God's presence bare, life becomes real, and we discover its fullness.

Who are you apart from money, titles, organizations, and fame? These false masks we wear steal our identity. Without them, I am *essentially defined*. I am ME. What freedom it is to know that at the core of my being, I am HIS. HE gives me value. HE gives me worth. Yes, at the quintessential depth of my soul, I am valued more than I could ever imagine. More than any title or rank could ever exalt me to.

Those titles and positions were a hoax that I believed. How about you? As I climbed up the ladder of success, my worth was determined by status and false idols. A striving to achieve and believe me, I was dying in the process. My drive and determination to do more . . . more . . . more rendered me exhausted and my well ran dry. Are you listening? Do you feel it too?

You are worth more than this. You are loved by a Redeemer. A Father who wants to give you rest. A Father who values you for YOU. Take that in. Breathe. You are precious, loved, important, exalted, and so worth it!

Stop reading for a moment and find the nearest mirror. Look at yourself and say these words: "I am worth it!" Say them over and over. Speak them into existence. As you see the windows of your soul looking back at you, are you acutely aware that He is there, whispering these words to you? Where have you been not to hear Him before now?

What I found was that without all the expectations—the hurdles to climb, people to please, limitless demands that others and myself made on me—I was finally *free*. Bare and unafraid. The past hurts and pains had slipped away into memories. Free. Free to explore who I am and what defined my life. Why I am here? And why He had made me uniquely me.

Start bare. Defining your existence begins with understanding yourself at the core of who you are. What makes you light up? What makes you laugh? When do you feel most like yourself? When do you say to yourself, *this is when I am happiest?* When you're _____ (you fill in the blank with an activity), all is right with the world. It's then that you are on the way to defining your existence.

Defining your existence has nothing to do with money, titles, organizations, or fame. It is who we are at the core of our beings. It is what makes us uniquely us. Once discovered, we can't help but be this person.

I have spent years in search of this basic question. Many people along my journey would say, "You know your purpose." I always wanted to respond, "No, I don't. Tell me what it is." It eluded me. I didn't understand. What was I blind from not seeing?

In the end, it was so obvious. It was right in front of me the whole time. How often do we complicate the obvious? Making something that is so apparent complex, dubious, an enigma. When, in fact, it has been right before us all along. Those others on my journey weren't so far off from the truth. I only had to open my eyes.

My big reveal: *I live to help others.* Simple, I know. But it is the truth. I can't help myself. My soul burns for opportunities to help others find happiness, live abundantly, and feel loved. It's what lights me up. Helping others see the specialness and beauty inside them is at the core of me.

I remember when I was in my twenties, waiting for a friend in the hospital parking lot. I saw an elderly woman walking. She was all alone, obviously going to a medical appointment. Every part of me wanted to walk alongside her, to join her on her journey. To give her reassurance and let her know that someone cared. Why was she alone? Why in this critical time of need did she not have someone walking alongside her, caring for her? And what could I do about it?

There are so many questions like these circling my mind throughout each day: Why are children suffering? Who is there when they cry out at night to hold them? Why are animals hurt by those they trusted to care for them? Why are people harming one another? Why does the color of our skin, our religious beliefs, or our social statuses matter? Why can't we all just love one another, accept each other, and try to understand each other?

I could go on and on about the injustices I see every day that tear at my soul. Why? Because He made me to see the pain He sees and give it a voice—to let everyone know what He sees. And I cannot afford to be silent anymore. My existence is defined by letting you know you are loved; you are valued and, my desire is to help you find happiness and live life abundantly. It's who I am.

When we are brave enough to be bare, we discover that we are worth more than we ever imagined or dreamed of. We are "less than" *no more*.

Jump in. Take this leap with me. And enjoy the exciting journey to the mountain top that awaits you . . .

At your core, who are you?

- What do you think about?
- What do you care about?

- If money or titles didn't matter and you could do anything, how would you spend your time?
- What lights you up?
- What brings you joy and happiness?

This is the truth that will set you free.

Chapter 2

PERMISSION

I am a people pleaser to my core. Self-described as the eternal "golden retriever" that sits by, waiting for that pat on the head, and loyal to the core. How many of you can relate? We are the responsible ones—often sitting with our heads down, deep into work, doing everything we are supposed to do while others are sitting by, idling chatting, or living it up with not a care in the world. I have always been this way. I was the child that when my sisters were goofing off, having fun, or doing nothing at all, I would be cleaning the house to help Mom—all for that surprise Mom would receive when she walked through the door. "An angel came and visited me" she would say when she got home from work. It would be that pat on the head of praise that compelled me to do it again or outdo myself the next time to get even more praise.

Fast forward to entering the workforce where I was always trying to take the initiative by doing more than my counterparts, to get the acknowledgments and praises from my boss. I was outstanding . . . or so I've been told.

Yet this perpetual self-reliance on others' praises also led me to a vicious cycle of needing others' permissions. Whether it was that discriminating boss whom I would never get permission to do things because I would not accept his sexual advances or the women bosses that would not give me praise because they saw another beautiful and talented woman as a threat to their next move toward the top.

I've learned a hard lesson. The truth is that **permission must come from within.** First, we must approve of ourselves: our talents, accomplishments, capabilities, and shortcomings. We must give ourselves permission to be all of who we are—the good, the not-so-great, and everything between. If we want to live our best lives, we must give ourselves permission to shine.

STEP ONE: BE OPEN

One day, I was in Starbucks, talking to my best friend. I was at a place in my life where I simply wanted more. I was a single mom to a beautiful four-year-old little boy.

I had a good job with enough money to pay the bills. We were doing fine, but life felt empty. Every day, I went through the motions: to bed, wake up, go to work, go home, go to bed, rinse and repeat. I loved and treasured my life with my son; I liked my job, yet I needed more.

My life lacked meaning. What was this all for? What was the end result? Could life really be about day-to-day existence? In Starbucks that day, I felt my soul come alive when in my moment of weakness, my brain stopped thinking and my soul spurted out a long-held desire. "I want my life to mean something. I want to stand for something. At the end of my life, I want to leave a legacy for my son, a legacy that will let him know that his mom stood for something and made a difference in this world." I was pouring my soul out to my friend and speaking unabashed truth.

And that's when it happened. A gentleman came over to my friend and me, excused himself for inter-rupting us and eavesdropping, and let me know he had overheard us talking.

"Will you come to [my place of employment] and take a tour?" He worked at an organization that served people with disabilities.

Of course, I said "Yes!"

At that moment, my universe changed. I went on that tour, was offered a job, ... and turned it down to make more money somewhere else.

But a year later, I would be offered another job with that same nonprofit, and destiny would be revealed.

Do you understand what was happening? I was trying to silence God. I wasn't listening. I was actively "doing my own life my way" while God was trying to get my attention. I was focused on the wrong thing—namely the almighty dollar. But God knew my heart and why He created me. God doesn't let go of our destinies, even when we at first say no. It was during this second chance that I started my career in the nonprofit industry. A decision that would change the trajectory of my life forever.

When you put your true self out there, it invites others to see you in that light, activating an opportunity to live out who God created you to be.

The moral of the story: be open. Open to exploring who it is you were meant to be. Open to what matters to you. There is a reason why you act, think, and behave the way you do. You were made to be uniquely you.

Innately, we all bring value. The point is, are you living out the value that He created you for? Or is it being masked by other things that are more important to you? Things like the quest for money, a certain lifestyle, a title, socioeconomic status, or a group of friends? What is holding you back from living your authentic self? Be open and let the possibilities flow. What would happen if you really did live the life that you were *meant* to live? Whose life would be changed in the process? What would your impact be? And what would be the rippling effect on others that only *you* were able to create to be for them? Are you going to live into that or hide that under a bushel (Matthew 5:15) for no one else to see? What happens when we step into our true selves, our true identity, and are open about who we really are and what truly matters in our life?

STEP TWO: DON'T UNDERESTIMATE YOURSELF

I learned a very difficult truth years ago on my way to finding out who I really was. In a nutshell, here is this truth: we *all* have the potential for greatness. If only we will simply believe it. The saying goes, "What would you attempt to do, if you knew you would not fail?" But the truth is, for many, they do not include themselves in this question. The underprivileged, the minority, those born without means, the immigrants, the forgotten, the abused. Are these words true for them? The truth is *yes*! Our value and worth are born within us. We live them each day. But it is our belief in our value and worth that either gives us a green light to soar or puts iron bars around the framework of our lives within which our belief system is formed.

Yet sometimes, we meet people in our lives that challenge our beliefs of ourselves. Teachers, mentors, family members, acquaintances, and yes, even strangers can redefine our view of ourselves. Again, God does not let go of our destiny.

My random encounter came when I was dating a man who was the president of his own company. We had been out on a few dates. During this time, we got to know each other and talked about work and our everyday lives. During these conversations, one night he asked me, "Why are you not a president of a company or a CEO?" I was taken aback by that question. *What? Are you kidding?* Who, me? Why on earth would you ask me that question? Me? A project coordinator. A single mom. A "just barely getting by" with her finances woman who was trying her best to raise a child on her own and keep a roof over both of their heads. *Me?*

And that's when he said it: "Yes, *you.*" He went on to say, "A talented, smart, quick-thinking woman who is the brightest in her company, and she knows it. The person who is running the show. The woman who is infinitely capable of doing and being so much more. Yes, you."

It was at that moment that God planted a seed. A seed that would take years to grow. This conversation would begin to nurture a root system within me, one that would eventually pop its little head up into the light. Like a planted seed, before it ever grows into the beautiful rose bush it was always meant to be. Yet this man saw the potential before him and dared to ask the question, "Why are you not _____?" (Fill in the blank for yourself.)

Who do you know that needs to hear these words? Or are these words for you?

- Who is that diamond that is ready to sparkle, yet is being hidden from the world?
- Do you continue to say nothing, or do you speak up and tell people what you see?
- Are you someone who pushes down the talent you see in others so your talents aren't usurped? Or so that you will be recognized instead?
- What would your life look like if you dared to be a voice for others?
- Are you open to receiving the blessings that come from helping others thrive?

When you put your true self out there, it opens the door to inviting others into the conversation.

STEP THREE: LEAP AND THE NET WILL APPEAR

There is an old saying: "Nothing ventured, nothing gained." When I think about my career, there have been several positions that I've begun and thought "This was a bit of a leap of faith." The thoughts inside my head continued, "I don't know how this is going to work out. Will I be a success or a failure? Was this the right move or not?" **The truth is, you are only a failure if you never try.** And doubt will kill your spirit.

To think we are the knowers of everything is foolish. The truth is that you know yourself. William Shakespeare said it best. "To thine own self be true." If you will bring your talent, fearless passion, energy, and attitude to learn, you will succeed. Permit yourself to *shine*!

Shining is a process. It begins at the crossroads of choice. First, we must pay homage to fear and doubt, which are also present at this juncture. They are the "takers" that rob us of our true potential. We must acknowledge them before we take any journey on our road to greatness, fulfillment, and happiness. There will always be roadblocks, potholes, pit stops, and hurdles present. No road is a smooth, easy road.

At the crossroads, before we even begin our leap, is a major roadblock. It is the roadblock of *fear*. Fear is real. As I've struggled with different fears throughout my life, it is a subject I know all too well. While fear is defined as an "unpleasant emotion" or "a feeling of anxiety," anyone who has struggled with fear will tell you that fear can be more than uncomfortable, at times even debilitating. It can grow to a point where it handicaps people, holding them hostage from living their best lives. I know; I've been there.

At this point, I must say that I wholeheartedly advocate for therapy and counseling, finding those who love us through our fears and who help us breathe through them, learn from them, laugh at them, and conquer our "fear mountains." What I've found is that if you'll do the work, on the other side of fear is unimaginable joy, confidence, and freedom.

For those brave souls who will push past their fears, confidence is waiting on the other side. You will have the ability to stand tall and speak your truth, whatever that is. Through battling fear, you get to know yourself very well. Embrace all of you with the freedom to "be" what you are passionate about.

At some moment in time, we have all come to this crossroads of choice. Do we take that job? Do we go after our dreams? Do we get on that airplane? Do we conquer our fear of driving down that highway alone for the first time? Do we push past our fears or succumb to them? Fear can either handicap us for life or propel us forward to our next step. The crossroads of choice is all of ours.

I would urge you to *leap!* The net will appear! I have leaped throughout my life. In my career, some of my favorite "shining moments" began with that utterly sick feeling in my stomach, my heart racing, and my brain asking, "What have you done now?" As I've left longstanding, stable positions for the wilderness and the unknown, I have learned that "leaping" reaps many rewards, and the cost of what you miss out on if you don't leap is way too high. Leaping allows you to learn new skills, the feeling of accomplishing new goals, problem-solving practice, self-reliance, and the confidence found in the knowledge that *you can* achieve far greater than you ever thought or imagined. Leaping says that you are bold and will let nothing come between the beauty of your dreams and your ability to achieve them.

Will you be knocked down along the way? Of course! We all have been and will continue to land awkwardly. Sometimes the scrapes and bruises are painful and even take time to heal. But as my mom always told me, "Your true power is not in how often you get knocked down but in how fast you get back up, dust yourself off, and keep moving forward." She was a very wise woman.

So how do you take the first step to leap? Leaping involves knowing your inner self, what you desire, and having the courage to go for it. Ask yourself: *What keeps me up at night?* What is that voice in the back of your head telling you to do? What are the things you can't live without? If you could dream crazy-big dreams, what would you be doing? You are the only person that can make your dreams a reality. No one can do it for you, and there is absolutely no substitute for hard work and going after your dreams.

There seems to be this school of thought today that says, "If I want something, I can have it." I believe that to be true. But it must be said that people who "have it all" have usually worked very hard to get what they wanted. They've put in the long hours, the effort, the thinking and planning, and the diligence to make their dreams a reality. The bigger the dream, the harder a person must work to achieve it. In other words, nothing worthwhile comes easily. Successful people, generally speaking, have a few things in common: hard work, determination, and they never give up on their dreams. Summed up, it's called *grit*.

Ask yourself: what are you willing to do to go after your dream? What is the risk of not going after your dream? Living a life of regrets is difficult. What is the consequence of not living your dream and not going for it?

STEP FOUR: SHINE

You've been open to possibilities and stepped into who you were meant to be. You've swung from the branches to dream higher than you ever thought you could, accomplishing goals as you lean into your dream. You've pushed past the fears to make that leap and realized that not only is there a net, but you will soon learn there are champions who will support you along the way (Chapter 7). So what's next?

Next is one of the simplest yet most complex hurdles that you will meet. It's the space to give yourself permission to shine.

Somehow, it is an oxymoron. We're finally on our way to achieving our dreams and what do we find? "We" are the ones holding us back. Yes, seeing is not always believing. Years ago, I was training for a half-marathon. Initially an untrained runner, I aspired to run well. I dreamed of being one of those graceful women who jutted forward, like a gazelle, effortlessly. So I put on my running shoes, and the first block around the neighborhood was hard. I became breathless in no time. Yet I persevered.

I kept putting on my running shoes day after day. The blocks became miles underneath my feet and breathing became easier with each outing. Sure, I still had to slow my pace along the way, even walk at times, but I kept moving forward. **Forward movement is what life is all about.** I had a dream, and I was determined to achieve it. But what I found is that the more I ran, the louder the thoughts in my head became: "Who do you think you are? You are *not* an athlete. Who are you kidding?" Yet I was running. I was taking the action that defined the word runner. Sometimes, even when we are in the midst of success, we must remind ourselves that we *can* do it . . . that, in fact, we *are* doing it.

Sure, there will be challenges and setbacks along the way; we should expect them. I learned a long time ago, it is not about how many times we fall, experience failure, or get let down. Life is about the ability to get back up on our feet and *keep moving forward*. The beauty is in the ability to get back up, stand tall, and keep moving. Have you ever watched a baby taking their first steps? Time and time again, they fall, yet they quickly get back up on their feet and try again. Somehow, throughout our lives, we have learned to self-doubt. Who are we to dream? Who are we to ever believe we can?

My question is "Who are you *not* to believe and dream?" Permit yourself to shine. Permission to be that brilliant, successful person you know yourself to be. What are you waiting for? Go begin to shine!

- Is fear holding you back from accomplishing your fears? If so, what could be on the other side of your fear?

- What dream is pulling you forward?
- Are you ready to leap?

Permit yourself to *shine* today. Your life is waiting.

Chapter 3

UNAPOLOGETIC

I have lived my life being the apologetic one. "Sorry I hurt your feelings. Sorry that the situation went that way. Sorry you treated me terribly; I must have done something wrong to deserve it." *Sorry.* I'm sorry. Yet it was when I recently experienced a difficult situation that my attention turned to wondering, "Why am I the one that is always apologizing? I didn't do anything wrong."

It is in our weakness and most vulnerable conditions that we have moments of utter clarity and become strong.

STEP ONE: TAKE BACK YOUR POWER

I had been working for a difficult boss. I knew I was not alone. Other employees throughout our company had come to me to vent their frustrations about this person. They were equally challenged as they described their situations. They desperately needed advice about what to do. This "leader" held a position of authority in the company. Yet, despite their senior-level position, their actions were contradictory to the definition of a *leader*. This person had a horrible habit of screaming at others—belittling and berating them—and punishing those who dared to self-advocate or push back during their mistreatment. We all know these types of leaders who use their positions of influence to serve their own egos and need for self-importance. The power they have affords them a false authority and a *carte blanche* license to behave however they feel the situation warrants, without fear of judgment or reprimand.

Power placed in the hands of abusive and toxic people is a dangerous weapon.

It wasn't until the wee hours of the morning, after I had awoken from a nightmare in which this person was physically harming me, that I realized something had to be done. It wasn't just others who were struggling. I had to take back my power too.

I researched my boss's behavior—harassment, belittling, putting me down in front of others, micromanaging, bullying—and what appeared before me was astonishing. What I had been enduring had a name: toxic work environment. This kind of environment is often led by one person. They position themselves at the head, as an ugly snake that needs to be silenced.

What I realized at that moment was there was nothing wrong with me. *It was not my fault.* It was another person's bad behavior. I need not apologize. I had been giving my job my all. I had done everything that was requested. Yet my boss's behavior worsened; their list of demands was growing as the bar kept moving higher and higher. They were turning up the heat.

Toxic bosses are bullies by nature, and bullies never act alone. Bullies draw strength from numbers. They usually find the weakest members in the group and enlist them to their cause. In my case, one vice president became two senior leaders, and I was their sheep to the slaughter. That is . . . until the day I took back my power.

STEP TWO: RECOGNIZE THE FRAUDS

In retrospect, throughout this trauma-filled period, many lessons were learned. But one is so readily apparent, it must be stated clearly, to curb the chance that we miss it altogether.

***Never* make apologies for *being you*.**

That's right; you were created for a purpose by our heavenly Father. People that push you down mean to rob you of the very essence of who you were created to be.

Did you hear that? If someone does not appreciate you for who you are, they are not someone worthy of your time, energy, or resources. Each of us was made to be unique; there is no one like us on the entire planet. Even identical twins think individually, have different talents and abilities, and more. We were made to bring our unique selves to this world and make a difference. When we apologize for being ourselves, it is like admitting that there was somehow a mistake for us being a certain way. To reach our highest potential as a person, we must not pretend to be someone we are not.

We must use who we are, with the talents and abilities He gave us, to learn, achieve, and be our best. Yet we also recognize that true talents and abilities are not always recognized. It is difficult in a world where hierarchy is the rule of the day, where the "privileged" take precedence.

Privilege today takes many forms. Hundreds of years ago, privilege would have taken into consideration the family you were born into. Throughout the years, privilege has evolved. There is no doubt that today, factors also include the color of your skin, your socioeconomic status, the country you were born in, and your family's religious practices.

"Privilege" is *real*. Oxford Languages online defines it as, "a special right, advantage, or immunity granted or available only to a particular person or group." Today, we can even buy certain privileges. Consider the ability for one to join an association or a certain group. We can choose a particular college, join a sorority or fraternity, or even pay to become a member of a golf club or business group that affords us certain privileges and reputation. Yet when this privilege comes at the cost of pushing down or discriminating against others, it is not only wrong, it is a tragedy.

Privilege has always been about those who have conquered others and been given more power. With more power comes more wealth and influence, and the cycle continues as people rise to the top, leaving others at the bottom. Many "so-called leaders" are not more deserving, nor are they more talented. Many of these leaders are in the positions they are because of the privileges they have acquired. At times, they are the ones who have silenced others and bullied their way to the top.

These individuals haven't earned their roles; they've gained access to them while gaining allegiances along the way. They've built themselves up while spreading rumors and labeling those they've conquered as "different, odd, not talented, troublemakers, and more" in an effort to keep them "in line" and silenced into lowered positions.

It's unthinkable to responsible, hardworking, rule-abiding achievers like me. We are the sheep. The dutiful doers that do what we're told and perpetually strive to go above and beyond. We outdo ourselves to achieve more and more only to realize that our hard work and achievements may not be rewarded as those with privilege take responsibility for our work or use it as a weapon against us.

Make no mistake, these leaders will never portray the definition, qualities, or characteristics of a true leader. They are the "frauds." They may enjoy positions of power. In fact, they are like lions who bring others that think like them into their dens and speak out poorly against the sheep. They recognize and take advantage of the goodness, kindness, talents, and abilities of the sheep and then hate them for it. When the sheep get out of line or want to be recognized and move ahead, they stand ready to pounce and push them back. They have the backing of other lions and will silence those who get in their way. Why? Because they live threatened. Theirs is a fear of being outshined, outworked, and, in the end, seen as inadequate.

Your ability to bring *you*—your God-given talents, abilities, and achievements together with the confidence and belief in yourself—is the only thing that will make these frauds cower and move away. Even lions cower in the light of the fire. It is not easy. Stand firm in your integrity and know who you are. There are frauds all around you. But truth is on your side.

STEP THREE: ASK IF YOU ARE FOLLOWING OR LEADING

Equally threatening are influencers, those that defy the norm and use their voices to stand and speak loudly.

I was raised with the social graces of yesterday, in a time when people politely raised their hands, waiting for their turns to speak. People graciously listened and took in others' messages with great thought and reverence. Yet what has become prevalent today is the individual who usurps others with the loudest voice and a quest to be heard.

I came into this knowledge only by seeing it first-hand in action. These are the "leaders" that skip the line and refuse to wait for their turns. It is not that they are more talented. They are *loud*, period. They are fearless and boisterous and refuse to be silenced. In their own minds, they are brilliant. They have an insatiable appetite for publicity and the limelight. They have an insatiable hunger to be seen and heard. These influencers are dangerous because they also attract followers.

Have you recognized that "followers" simply follow? To these influencers, because of their volume, people listen and gather around them to see what the noise is all about. Before long, a group has gathered. People want to be part of the "in crowd." Soon, this "leading" person is heralded as brilliant; after all, look at their following.

Yet no one has truly listened to "their voice" and the message behind what they are spewing. I have seen this time after time. For the analytical person like me, you can tear apart their message as perhaps disgruntled, uninformed, born of poor judgment—a host of reasons. Yet many take the information at face value and simply agree.

Are we really that naïve to follow without thinking? Without discerning if we agree with this person or accurately assess if they have an important message to share? Think about it: how many of us are following people just because they are out there seeking and getting the attention—tweeting about going to events, speaking at conferences—when there really isn't a platform of original thought upon which they stand?

Discernment is critical. Are we following to be a part of the "in" crowd? Or have we really looked into and under the points of the message before us to critique its content?

STEP FOUR: STOP APOLOGIZING AND BE YOU

Stand in your power. Each of us has a voice. For many of us, our voice will never be heard. It's not that our voice is unimportant; it's because our fear wins out. *Who am I to speak up, stand out, and push forward?* Fear of failing, the fear of the unknown, the fear of judgment, and all of the other countless fears that keep us silenced are exhausting. Isn't it time you stand for something you believe in?

If today is the day, then unapologetically take back your power and *lead*.

There is a saying, "If not you, then who?" Another is "nothing ventured, nothing gained." Whatever hurdle is holding you back, isn't it time to make the leap? The world is waiting for you. Be *silent no more.*

Who is taking your power or quieting your voice?

- Who are you following? Do you agree with the message they stand for? Or are you following because they are making the loudest noise?
- Are you standing up to speak your truth? If not, why not?
- Who needs to hear your voice of truth?
- What truth do you stand for?

Chapter 4

SET FREE

(FROM FEAR TO TRIUMPHANT)

**Then they cried to the Lord in their trouble,
and He saved them from their distress.
He brought them out of darkness, the utter
darkness, and broke away their chains.
Psalms 107: 13-14**

What is the one barrier in your life that keeps you from achieving all that you were meant to be? It's a heavy question, I know. Thinking back on my life, my barrier was so apparent. It was in front of me the whole time. In fact, it ruled me. What I'm about to share with you is *raw*. It was, unquestionably, the most painful time in my life. To even utter its existence comes with deep scars, secrets, and regrets. It's that time in your life that you'd rather forget and deny ever happened. We say to ourselves, "it was a different life ago" to help ease the pain. It was a time so desperate, that you perhaps still want to disassociate with it and pretend it doesn't exist.

Is it possible for your greatest trial to be one of your biggest blessings? I look back on this time and know that it was this moment that I was saved for. It is this suffering that God wants me to tell. The story of "My Life" arose out of this time. One could say that this time *made* me. Because through the pain and scars, my world was changed and formed. Life experiences change how we view our world.

So I wonder, what part of your life are you hiding from? What secrets do you not want to be told? I offer another question: could this be your defining moment? Could it be "Your Story" that needs to be told?

- What are the defining moments in your life that need to be shared?
- What is God revealing through your story?

STEP ONE: IDENTIFY THE CHAINS THAT BIND US

Paralyzing fear is my secret. I've experienced fear and anxiety so profound that I've thought I'd lost my mind, my soul, my existence. I've been trapped within myself, not recognizing who I am, painfully trying to escape a mind that held me captive. Reading these words now, I remember feeling so lost, so alone and afraid. I was a shell of myself, and I didn't recognize "me" anymore. And I was too lost to even know how to get "me" back. Even the reading of these words brings back pain and despair as the mind never forgets what it has endured. Though merely words on a page, the memories are fresh, yet they no longer have power over me.

Now, read that paragraph above again, only this time imagine it is you talking—that you are the person experiencing this paralyzing fear.

This situation is *real* and *profound*. It was for me, and it is for many.

When your mind is not your own, when you are afraid of everything, including yourself, yet you are acutely aware of the fact that you are not okay and cannot fix what is happening, it is traumatizing. There might be times when you no longer trust yourself because your mind seems foreign to you. Yet you are aware, profoundly aware, of *everything* . . . of every sound: the tick of the clock on the shelf, the intakes of breaths of those around you, the shuffling of footsteps approaching. It's overwhelming.

I asked: How did my life get to this place? What happened? In a mere instant, my mind would become a foreign place—uninhabitable, even for me.

The medical diagnosis is post-traumatic stress disorder, or PTSD. For me, it was brought on by medical procedures and way too many prescription drugs to induce fertility. On one hand, it's honorable. I mean really. What lengths would you endure to get the one thing that you wanted the most—in my case, a child. Month after month, year after year . . . an endless journey with no reward in sight. And no explanation. Surgeries to fix what they thought was broken, only to find out that no, that wasn't the problem. The true culprit would be found years later.

The truth was . . .

God is sovereign. And He had a different plan.

I attribute my still being here on earth to one woman alone. A woman whose strength came from similar trials and losses. A woman whose compassion molded my life on so many levels, indescribable as she lived out her faith in God *every moment* of her life. I am blessed that she shared her faith with me, her daughter. It was my mom who saved my life.

I will never forget the moment I called her when my worlds collided. "I don't know how I am going to make it through the day!" She must have heard the sincerity, or maybe the fright in my voice.

In her soft, calm voice she replied, "Jody, just breathe." Then she said, "Jody, take baby steps. One step at a time. And breathe. *You will get through this.*" It was her willing me to live. I would heed her advice for the next five minutes.

Five minutes later, I was back on the phone. "I made it. What's next?"

She said again, in her slow and peaceful voice, breathing through every word, "Keep going . . . take baby steps. Five more minutes. It's going to be okay. You can do this . . ." How did she know what to say? She was walking me through my panic, uncertainty, and doubt. My frail self was beyond able to do this myself. I was grasping for and clinging to every word. My mom walked me through that whole day. Minute by minute, hour by painstaking hour. It was a day forever emblazoned in my soul. Like a tattoo, it has been carved into the framework of my life. It is a part of me—my make-up, my being.

I could have been checked into a stress center, or been hospitalized, drugged up to never return to me. Thank God for my mom. She was there. No one ever knew what I went through that day or the weeks and months that followed. I am a professional. I hid it well. Work was my haven, and I used it as an escape. It helped to pass the time. Time was my enemy. Feeling like this was something I wanted to quickly get through and get over. Time could not pass fast enough. I sought out anything to keep my mind focused on something else. The distraction of work was a lifesaver, something to keep me focused off me. Work was something I could do that I was good at. It was a known entity, and I felt safe. I had the love from my coworkers all around me. After seven years, we had become a family. Mom was two hours or a phone call away. So work became my lifeline.

Through my mom's reassurance, I knew that God was with me too. I had always heard, "He doesn't give you more than you can handle." Well . . . that is something that I could not believe at that moment. To this day, I still have my doubts. This season of fear and anxiety was bad and when I say that it literally took me to the end of myself, I mean every word. Perhaps what people truly mean is that He doesn't give you more than you can handle *without him*. With that, I would completely agree as God was my refuge and my strength. My mind was foreign and reeling, but He was not. Thoughts were constantly spinning out of control, but He was steady. I questioned, "Will I ever be the same again?" As the saying goes, "A mind is a terrible thing to lose." Trust me, it is, especially when you are the one who has lost it.

I couldn't see how "this moment" in my life would ever end. How would I survive? I asked, "What is my future? How can I keep going and enduring this excruciating mental pain day by day, moment by moment?" I was looking for the exit door, a way to go back to normalcy. I wanted to fix what was going on inside of my head. I wish I could tell you that it came quickly, that I snapped back to normal days later. I remember my counselor saying that in a year or two it would be better. WHAT? I knew I couldn't stand this feeling for a moment—let alone for years. I wouldn't make it! But then she said the words that I needed to hear: "It won't be like today always. It will get better. Each day will be better, and over time, this will all be a memory."

Please remember this, if nothing else from this entire book:

Hope is a *powerful* thing.

And did I need hope! I needed it like the body needs air and food to live. How was I going to "make it" through this time? It was the question always in my mind. Yet I've learned a very powerful lesson.

***Never* underestimate the power of God.**

God is always there, walking with us. I know that some of you are doubting this. You're asking, "Is He real?" or saying, "Sure, sure . . . that's nice to say, but . . ." I know it sounds cliché. But it is true. *He lives.* Someone once asked me how my faith got so strong. They said, "It's like you know God is there, without question." I spoke with such authority about Him. How did I know? How was I sure?

When you walk through fire and aren't burnt, you know *He is real.*

When you see God's hand in action through every aspect of your life, you know, He is there. When you feel an angel touch your back and no one is in the room, you know they were heaven-sent for that moment. And one day, when I was at the end of myself with nowhere to turn, God got my attention through a book. I was walking through Walmart when a stack of discounted books got my attention. At the time, I wasn't an avid reader, so it's not like I was looking for books. But there it was on the pile, "Making Miracles," written by Arnold Fox and Barry Fox. It drew my attention. I needed a miracle; I was beyond desperate for one. And this book became it.

God saved my life through this book. It was His voice that I heard as He taught me to calm myself and listen for His gentle voice. He reassured me that He was there through its loving message . . . and my current circumstances. He gave me hope that I could get better if I would try my best, engage in the practices within, and trust Him. The book was about living in God's stillness and practicing belief in Him, and day by day, my life got brighter and joy returned.

My anxiety calmed and over time, my body stopped shaking. I journaled daily through this season. What I wrote was too hard to bear reading back, but I bore my soul through my letters to God. In one letter, I spoke of shaking so hard I feared my body would rip apart. I had been very ill, dropping weight like crazy, and had to make myself eat. Even the thought of food made me sick and seemed more than I could bear. The love from a good therapist made me continue as she confirmed, "Just try."

I say all of this to let you know that there are *no obstacles* that will keep God's love from you, ever. He loved you before you ever knew Him. And He chose *you*, above His own life, to save. He would go to the ends of this earth, and has, for you. It is we, mere humans, who put boundaries on God. We persuade ourselves into believing that He doesn't exist. That He couldn't possibly love us if He only knew . . .

Believe me. He does know. And He loves you regardless. I know because I've experienced His love. Still, even in the knowing, we tend to push God away. We tell ourselves that we've got this, we can do it on our own.

Now, let me ask you: "How low do you have to go, and how much despair and pain must you be in before you'll turn to Him?"

- What is it going to take for you to believe in God and let Him in to help heal you?
- How long can you go it alone?
- Does He have your attention yet?

As I got my life back and my mind became my friend again, I realized that fears had developed and become my crutches. I had endured so much pain that it was like my mind was trying to prevent "it" from happening again. If only I was more cautious; if only I didn't push the boundaries; if only I could just "be safe," *it* wouldn't happen again. I would do anything not to relive this pain, to keep this from ever happening again, to keep it at bay. Fears and the need to control my life and my surroundings brought me protection from the world around me, protection from all of the unknowns. Anything that I could do to keep control over my life, I instituted. My obsessive-compulsive (OCD) habits that ensued were ridiculous. I was checking to make sure things were "off" so nothing bad would happen. Checking that the blinds were turned a certain way in the house because, in my mind, that was what was needed to prevent something bad from happening. Crazy, I know. Welcome to my world (wink).

My "miss" was ever believing that, somehow, I could control the world around me. As humans—and I must tell the truth here—we are slow learners. Yet thanks be to God, He never gives up on us. But this does beg the question: What lengths do you go to "control" your world? Maybe it's keeping up appearances and buying nice clothes, dining at certain restaurants, joining the country club, living in the exclusive community, or getting the Lexus SUV you've always wanted.

These false securities mislead us into believing that we're fine, that we've got this. We're in control. Don't get me wrong, there is nothing wrong with having these things. However, we must know that our true safety comes from God alone. God is in control. He is the only one that is ever in control. And He is the only "safety net" we need to hold onto in this world.

STEP TWO: LEARN THE LESSONS

I have come a long way since this season many years ago. I look back on these years, and they are but a memory. However, I also recognize the multitude of gifts this period brought me: my relationship with God, my resiliency and steadfastness, and the need to give hope, encouragement, and grace—just as I was given these gifts through Him. I learned not to judge. Trust me that you don't know what someone else is going through. There may be more to the story than you could ever imagine.

While I would *never* want to go through that trial again—even today, the trauma is so real that I believe I barely made it through last time—I know God was molding me, growing me, and allowing me to see things through His perspective, His lens. He taught me one of the greatest gifts, humility. He slowed me down. I have always been a self-described worker and do-er. So He slowed me down to almost a full stop. During this time in my life, I would have normally been busy doing my life. This period of time instead became my *focus* time. The time I needed to center myself on Him, draw closer to Him, and understand clearly what really matters in life. This season changed my perspectives about suffering and the pain people are experiencing. It helped me become *real*. To let go of the facades that don't matter. It helped me become relatable . . . because, believe me, when I say I understand, I mean it; I *understand* pain, suffering, and mental illness. I understand the images that go with mental illness and the need for society to realize it is sickness, and we need to view it as such. Today, I have learned that my illness was brought on by taking too many infertility drugs, having back-to-back surgeries, and not having the support I needed to take care of myself. I was pushed to the brink and eventually, over the edge. I now know that when people say, "You know yourself best," it's true. We need to trust ourselves instead of seeking the approval of others.

How long must any of us seek the approval of others instead of approving ourselves?

- What are the lessons that God is trying to teach you?
- What are you suffering from that you need to let go of and let God?
- What are you trying to control that you are grasping to maintain a grip on?

STEP THREE: MOVE FROM FEAR AND BE SET FREE

Have you ever wanted to do something so badly, yet you didn't know how you were going to accomplish it? For me, traveling to Italy was my desire, a long-held bucket list item that I had always dreamed of. "One day, I'll go to Italy!"

The moment we booked our tickets, fear came along for the ride. Negative anticipation of the unknown enveloped me. Would I freak out on the plane as we flew over the ocean? What if I wanted "off" the flight after a few hours into it? Once the doors closed, there was no turning back. It was a one-stop flight. And what if I got there and needed to go back to safety (America) because I just couldn't stand not feeling "safe?" These were some of the thoughts reeling in my head. As our flight date approached, I gave my husband one instruction, "Don't leave without me. Make sure I'm on that plane. Even if I say no, get me in the seat." And I was serious.

When the actual day came upon us, no one would have ever known there had been even one worry in my head. I walked on the plane like a pro.

**God answers prayers
when we ask, seek, and find Him.**

Proverbs 3:5 instructs, "Trust in the Lord with all your heart and lean not on your own understanding." Full of fear yet with a prayer to bring peace—and yes, even joy—through this adventure, I found more than I ever would have imagined. I found freedom.

My desire to go to Italy must have been heaven-sent. For when I put everything on the line and trusted Him, He came through. I was completely in His hands. I had control of nothing—not the flight or this new land I was approaching, not the new culture. Nothing was familiar. I found myself again a foreigner. Yet this time, I knew that God was with me. He was by my side and enjoying watching me in my newfound freedom, making discoveries at every turn. Italy became the perfect destination as God revealed the place to me where his disciples once stood. I felt him throughout the journey. From the brick-lined streets to the waters of the canals and to the generosity of its people, God was basking in my every delight.

Italy was indescribably beautiful. The columns, arches, handcrafted wood, and stonework of history unfolded as we learned about the buildings and the ancient peoples. The craftsmanship that surrounded us was beautiful beyond words. But nothing compared to the statue of David. The sculpture of David tells the story about my life, and your life, and reveals God in so many ways, showing the depths of His love for each of us, as well as His grace and mercy.

The story of how David was created has been shared through the years. As the legend goes, many artisans were asked to create a famous masterpiece out of this piece of marble. Many failed. They said the marble was too hard, too *unworkable*. Then, at twenty-six years of age, Michelangelo accepted the challenge with enthusiasm. Michelangelo, it is said, was a man of faith. I can only imagine the conversations that he had with our Lord. As David slowly revealed himself, coming out of the stone, it became this breathtakingly beautiful masterpiece. When asked how he created David, Michelangelo said, "I didn't. David was always in there. I just chipped away all of the pieces that weren't David." I love this.

It paves the way for us to ask ourselves—as we are each a masterpiece—"What are the limiting beliefs that we carry about ourselves that hold us back from our true potential and need to be chipped away?" As I was enjoying my newfound freedom throughout Italy, I realized the correlation between David and my life. David was always there, on the inside. Yet he was weighted down by the things around him that weren't him. When these were chipped off, the true beauty of David was revealed . . . and it became a masterpiece. For me, fear had ruled my life. It had surrounded me for as long as I could remember. The fear of not having enough money, of losing a loved one, of not being good enough, and fear for my safety and security. The list goes on and on. Yet here I was, in a foreign land, embracing *life* with no guardrails or crutches to reign me in. I was on God's time and enjoying freedom triumphantly, like a toddler exploring their newfound freedom.

Living into the trueness of who you were created to be involves a hard look at the beliefs that are holding you back. Beliefs that you were raised with, such as you're not good enough, you're not smart enough, you're poor, you don't have enough money, your skin color defines who you are, and so on. Yes, all of these beliefs are a part of your story. But there is a reason you have the story that you do. As the Bible says about God, "For you created my inmost being; you knit me together in my mother's womb" (Psalm 139:13). It is not by accident that you've had the life you were given. It is for God's purpose.

So what will you allow Him to do with it? Our lives are not our own. They are His. And when you let go and let God, you will be truly *set free*.

Since Italy, I've been set free. I think about all of the times that I held myself back with a belief that I couldn't or shouldn't do something. I was scared and afraid, instead of trusting God. It is we who limit ourselves and our abilities. It says in Romans 8:31, "If God is for us, who can be against us?" God wants us to enjoy our life and not to worry. "Can any one of you by worrying add a single hour to your life?" (Matthew 6:27). God wants us to live all-out, trusting in Him. He will supply everything we need. It says so in Philippians 4:19: "And this same God who takes care of me will supply all your needs from his glorious riches, which have been given to us in Christ Jesus."

Living in the trueness of who you were created to be unlocks the true potential within you. And when we accept ourselves in the fullest manner, we are able to share ourselves with others and bring the impact for which we were created and meant to share with this world.

This reminds me of one of my favorite poems by Marianne Williamson, "Our Deepest Fear" which says, "Our deepest fear is not that we are inadequate. Our deepest fear is that we are powerful beyond measure."

I used to think that love was conditional. If only I was ten pounds thinner; if only I were more beautiful; if only I made more money or lived in a nicer house in *that* area of town. Professionally, I thought, if only I were smarter like so-and-so. How often do we try to "prove" who we are instead of "being" who we were created to be? Be the person that you are searching for, and you will find others start wanting to emulate you.

So whatever your story is, whether you are smart or not so smart, talented or not so talented, rich, or poor . . . regardless of the color of your skin, your ethnicity, your sexual orientation, or preference—gay, straight, bi or trans—*we* are *all* God's children. The good news is that He loves us. Now we need to love and embrace ourselves. We are unique and wonderfully made. None of us was an accident. We were created exactly as He wanted us to look, with our unique traits and talents, and for and with a purpose. Now go live into that.

Be brilliant. Be *free*, free from the approval of others and from the burden of needing to control your entire life. Let go of the guilt, shame, regrets, pain, and sorrows. Let go and let God.

And for your newfound perspective, I will tell you one more thing I've learned. Sometimes, being a foreigner is a blessing. Embrace it. It releases us from the chains of the past and allows us to embrace *all* of ourselves—our talents, our gifts.

Just be you.

- Where in your life have you underestimated God?
- If fear wasn't holding you back, what God-sized goal would you set out to accomplish?
- If you could be anything, what would you dream to be?

Now, go live *that.* Leap and the net will appear.

Chapter 5

BECOMING QUEEN AND KING

(CLAIMING YOUR LEGACY)

Life is not about you. Life is about others.

Each of us, upon arrival in this world, was made for a purpose. God assures us of this when David said, "He knit us together in our mother's womb" (Psalm 139:13). He gave each of us the qualities and characteristics we are supposed to have. I often thank God for the parents He gave me—for giving me a mother and father who truly loved God and were devoted to Him. This fact alone set my life on a trajectory to serve to our Lord.

The day I was born, like most of you, my parents named me. I am blessed to be named after my mom,

Joy Diane. Take her name Joy and add the "D" from Diane, and it makes Jody. Then she gave me her mother's middle name, Lee, to complete this dynamic duo. Jody Lee—a name given for a purpose, to honor two women and communicate, *you are a part of us.*

Names are important. They help to define us. They begin to tell the story of who we are. Many names are given for the heritage behind them. It's a "family name," a parent would say. "You were named after Grandpa John or Grandma Elizabeth." Some names are given to remind us of the times or important memories. My son, Graham, was named after a beloved person in our lives, a person who, although he was a young adult at the time, was kind, helpful, giving, and lived to serve others. He wanted to be a doctor to help others. I couldn't help but believe that when we named Graham, he would follow in this young man's footsteps and have that kind of character. Today, that wish has come true as Graham is all these things and more. Graham's name was given in honor and love. When I meet a person named Grace, I often think of her parents and the blessing of God that she must be to them. I believe many of our names were meant to be. Yes, our parents bestowed our names, but I believe that our Lord inspired them. After all, God named each of the species in the world; to each, He gave a name.

Joy. My mom's name was given to her with a purpose in mind. Anyone who knew her would tell you that her name fit her perfectly and that she fulfilled the meaning of her name through and through. As she would have told you:

J is for Jesus
O is for Others
Y is for Yourself

And Y is last for a reason.

My mom was His. She lived her life to follow Him. Period. Next came others. My mom lived to serve. She was the most selfless person I have ever met. Her happiness truly came as the result of being in service to others. It is what she lived for.

I share this bond as her namesake. From my earliest memories, I've heard His calling on my life. I have always aspired to be "His." I live to do good and to serve too. I remember standing up in a Sunday evening service as a child, giving a testimony of what the Lord had done for me that week. I'm sure my sisters were rolling their eyes! *Who does she think she is?*

I had an insatiable yearning to be close to God and to please Him. Bedtime in our house would involve Mom tucking us in and me praying for everyone.

After the lights went out, one by one, I would bless my household.

"Goodnight, Mom. I love you and will pray for you."

"Good night, Jill. I love you and will pray for you."

One by one until I heard, "Jody, go to bed." True story. It's a wonder I'm still alive, and my sisters didn't do me in.

Defining who you are goes far beyond your name, though. It begins with knowing who you are *and* the message you are meant to be to this world. So let me pause here and ask you:

- What are those things that gnaw at you?
- What keeps you awake at night? (There is your starting point.)
- If you could tell the world one thing, what would it be?

When I think back to the day at Starbucks that changed my life, the day when God allowed someone to hear my voice, I know that I was speaking my truth. I was *silent no more*. I was speaking from the depths and yearnings of my soul, and God was listening.

My declaration was to stand up and be heard; simply put, it was a desire to matter. I wanted my life to stand for something. To be His. To begin living a life that mattered, a life that gave me purpose. It was a desire that was born out of a deep-seated yearning to have my world make sense.

I remember many times trying to understand this life. For years, I would look up at the heavens and the stars at night and question God. "Is this *it*, Lord? Surely this merry-go-round life couldn't be all that we were designed for. Could it be?"

This getting up to go to work, driving myself all day for the almighty paycheck, coming home to eat dinner, and going to bed to do it all over again the next day. There was something seriously missing, producing a deep yearning inside me to understand God's purpose for and presence in my life. I desired to be used. To come into the fullness of being His servant and have His purpose fulfilled through my life. Once you find your purpose, your life will have new meaning, and you won't want to live any other way.

It begins by understanding your voice.

STEP ONE: FIND YOUR VOICE

There are many people whom I've admired throughout my life—women who I've aspired to be like. If you were to ask me who is the *one* woman I'd like to most emulate, one woman comes to mind and rises to the top of the list. I want to be like Princess Diana.

In my mind, Princess Diana was the epitome of love and grace, fearlessness with resounding courage. People were attracted to her beauty and her position within the monarchy. After all, what little girl doesn't have dreams of growing up to be a princess? Walt Disney built a legacy upon this dream. But for me, this attraction went deeper.

I was attracted to Princess Diana, not only for her beauty—inside and out—but for her *substance*. She mattered. Her platform was centered on helping the less fortunate and giving a voice to those who were voiceless. She was instrumental in starting conversations that changed the attitudes and perspectives of millions around the world on important issues, such as HIV/AIDS, leprosy, and land mines to name a few. Images come to mind, like the picture of her wearing her boots in a war zone as she brought attention to the dangers of land mines. Or the picture of her with a sick child cradled in her arms. She had blazon strength to persevere despite what others thought. Why? Because she had discovered her genuine and authentic voice. She knew what truly mattered in life, and she knew it was her responsibility to give voice to the injustices she saw all around her. It was her time to tell the stories. She used her influence as a princess to help lend her voice to causes that mattered. Over her lifetime, Princess Diana built a legacy of care, compassion, kindness, and strength while inspiring nations to take action and follow in her footsteps. She set a new standard for the Royals and inspired many. It is truly beautiful to see her sons follow in their mother's footsteps. They model her strength and voice as they carry their mother's torch forward and deepen the legacy and voices they, too, have been given.

So what would it look like if we were all queens and kings? What would you be known for? How would you serve others? What would be your platform for people to follow?

While queen or king may never be your official title, is it really that far-fetched to believe that we don't have any influence over our world—or our portion of it? After all, we have influence over our families. One could say that generations are impacted by how we "rule" our family. As we teach the younger generations our values, character traits, and rules of conduct (e.g., to respect others, the compassionate treatment of others, how to treat women, and what kind of a leader to be), they are watching and learning. The popular holiday movie, *It's a Wonderful Life*, displays this scenario perfectly as the main character, George Bailey, discovers that if he never would have been born, many others who were impacted by his life would have also been changed. It demonstrates that one person's existence does have the capacity to change countless people's lives forever. Our life can have a positive effect—bringing good on those around us—or a negative effect—causing damage, even a devastating outcome—on the lives of others whom we encounter.

So if we are to be queens and kings in our places of the world, what standard do we hold ourselves to when contemplating the platform under which we serve? The duties of being a *sovereign*, according to The British Monarchist Foundation, are to "act as a focus for national identity, unity and pride; to give a sense of stability and continuity" (Glum, Julia. *International Business Times*, January 13, 2017).

While Princess Diana may never have officially become queen, she most definitely fulfilled this standard of conduct as a queen in the making. In doing so, she served her people well. We can all choose to live like queens and kings in the making.

- What voice or message would you establish that would bring identity, unity, and pride?
- What would you say to your followers to give them a sense of stability and continuity?
- What code of conduct would you hold yourself accountable to?

Each of us brings to this life our own unique lens through which we see and understand the world. From the moment we are born, our life events shape us, molding our belief systems, our perspectives about the world around us, and how we view our roles in the treatment of others. Even the most basic of ideals, such as how we are loved, how we are spoken to, if we are cherished, or if we can be discarded and abused are laid as a foundation early in our lives. Our daily lives, with our successes and trials, become our "Operating Guides," which train us to be the individuals we become. As the Bible says, "Train up a child in the way he should go and even when he is old, he will not depart from it" (Proverbs 22:6). And as Dorothy L. Sayers said, "God wastes nothing—not even sin."

Every single event in our life shapes and defines our views. How we view our experiences, especially as we mature and grow into adults, defines our realities. We learn that we have a powerful thing called *choice*. We can use our trials, pain, failures, and losses to strengthen us and make us more resilient, or we can focus on our difficulties and remain hostages to our memories forever. It is all within our choice. Choice moves us forward, knocks us back, or immobilizes us. I believe that God's intent for each of us is to build our voices to be blessings to others. As He reminds us in Isaiah 61:2–3, God can make beauty out of ashes.

If the choice is yours, then what will you choose? How can you use the events of your life to fulfill your life's purpose?

STEP TWO: BECOME A VOICE FOR THE VOICELESS

I knew a young lady once who had endured far too much for the young age she was. Her painful memories, starting with years of being sexually abused as a child, turned into deep-seated depression and anxiety in her early adulthood. The mental turmoil left unresolved scars throughout her mind and body that plagued her. In her twenties, these events manifested themselves into physical sickness—to the point of causing debilitating physical ailments. The evilness of what she had endured had plagued her body and mind to exhaustion.

Her life's story was defined by what had happened to her as her mind relived over and over again her perpetrators' actions, nearly every hour of her life. Upon meeting someone new, she would unload these memories; they were her story. Her story defined her existence. She was a prisoner. To anyone who would listen with empathy, love, and compassion, she would eagerly relive her story and tell of her still weeping scars.

Yes, it's horrible, evil, and tragic. Stories like this happen in this world. I wish I had the power to bring instant healing to those that have suffered so much at the hands of others. In some way, to undo the evil that had occurred (and continues to unfold) and make it better.

However, I believe we have a God who is bigger than all our suffering and who stands ready and waiting to heal us and show us His glory. The pain and scars don't have to be the endings to our stories, only parts of it.

Please understand that I am not saying or suggesting for a moment that we should just forget the trauma from our pasts, discount it as suffering, and move on. On the contrary: we know that even God weeps for the suffering of His children (Matthew 18:6, Romans 12:19). Instead, I believe God wants to use our stories to tell His story through our own. To tell of a God who loves us and can heal us from all of our pain and suffering. To tell a different story, one of His redemptive love. Yes, these things happened . . . but God!

"Behold, I am making all things new" (Revelations 21:5). God does not intend for us to suffer. I often think about what God could do with this young woman's story. How many people could she reach and bring hope to as she revealed His faithfulness in bringing her through this situation? She would be such an advocate for all women who suffer similar stories of sexual abuse by those they should have been able to trust. Her testimony would be so powerful. Her voice alone has the power to impact and change lives. Yes, those horrible things happened, but look at God. He is greater! Our pain and suffering are not the endings to our stories, but they can be the launching points for us to reveal, first-hand and with authority, that God brings true healing and makes beauty from ashes. He allows forgiveness, He heals, and He restores.

We have a responsibility as queens and kings to be bold, to rise up against fear, and take a stand for those who are not able to stand—for those who are waiting for us to step up into action.

And for those of you who have not endured such magnitude of pain, sorrow, loss, or fear—those who don't yet know the suffering of these emotions—perhaps you, too, could stretch and grow. As it says in Galatians 6:2, we are to "Carry each other's burdens, and in this way, you will fulfill the law of Christ."

We are responsible to each other. And those who have suffered greatly need people to lean upon for strength.

RESPONSIBILITY, ACCOUNTABILITY, AND TOLERANCE

In this day of social media, where everyone is "bearing all" across all platforms, from Facebook and Instagram to Twitter and others, without giving a second thought to the consequences, we must acknowledge that with using our voice comes much responsibility and accountability for our words. Our truth, which is one person's perspective, must allow for others' viewpoints. After all, even a monarchy employs staff for guidance and wise counsel.

I am thankful to the Lord that He has stretched my thoughts, ideas, and viewpoints—over the last few years, especially. In all things, we must seek to understand and to *stand under* the thoughts and views of others, to allow their voices to be heard alongside our own. Stepping into your voice comes with an understanding that tolerance for others' viewpoints must also be present. True leadership is not displayed by a leader who has to have it their way all of the time. That, in fact, is the definition of a dictatorship. True leadership is responsible for others, whereas a person accepts that there are consequences for their actions toward others.

Accountability of our words is equally critical. "But I tell you that every idle word that men shall speak, they shall give account thereof in the day of judgment." (Matthew 12:36, KJV). In other words, exaggerated talk is like nothingness. We must have meaning to the words we speak. We could probably all name a few people who enjoy having their faces and names in the limelight. They post on media to keep their "likes" up and their profile numbers high. Theirs is another battle. It is the battle for status and to be relevant. These people crave being seen and heard to such a high degree, they will do anything to self-promote and be recognized. They are in a constant battle with themselves and anyone they perceive to stand in their way of center stage. They have an insatiable appetite to self-promote so that people deem them as important and worthy.

To use your voice for selfish, self-seeking behaviors is not worthy of a queen or king. It misses the point entirely. Let us remember the first line of this chapter: *Life is not about you.*

Let's also remember this Scripture: "Let nothing be done through selfish ambition or conceit, but in lowliness of mind let each esteem others better than himself. Let each of you look out not only for your own interests, but also for the interest of others" (Philippians 2:3–4).

Armed with the uniqueness of who we are, our voices, and our genuine desire to bear one another's burdens, we can truly follow in the steps of some of the world's greatest leaders.

Becoming a queen or king involves putting the needs of others first—even above our own—remembering it is not position or rank that is of value but the ability to do good, unify, and bring stability and continuity to others. Once you have determined your unique voice, you are sure to leave a legacy worthy of a queen or king.

- How can the story of your life influence your voice?
- What events have occurred that might lay the foundation of your platform?
- How can you use your voice (as a queen or king) to bring unity, identity, and pride to others?
- Have you asked God how He wants to use your story to serve others?

Chapter 6

BE KIND AND DO GOOD

L ike a blazing tornado or a pop-up summer storm, in she walked. A five-foot-two powerhouse on heels, she was confident, accomplished, and obviously noteworthy. *What does she have that I don't?* I thought as she walked in the door. Why had they chosen her to be our next president? Sure, she had an impressive resume with all of the right accolades to follow. She had made a name for herself. But *what* did our board possibly see in her?

The story and truth would unfold over time. Wisdom gained always makes an indelible impact on one's life. The truth is, this woman would end up leaving her mark on my life. It is a truth that still resonates vibrantly today as it did when I first experienced it. Her story speaks a timeless message for all ages.

STEP ONE: LIVE YOUR TRUTH

Flawed—oh, unabashedly so and ashamed of nothing. She was imperfect and quirky. Many would scratch their heads and ask, "Why is she so successful? Why her?" Yet the truth in its purest form stood right before us. This woman was small in stature yet powerful beyond measure. The truth is, the person before me was a beautiful, magical person who was 100 percent *real* to the core and came with full transparency. Unashamed of anything, she lived her truth through and through. She was genuine, smart, hard-working, and generous. She would give you the shirt off her back before you ever thought to ask for it. She would often bring in special gifts to her staff. Why? Because the truth was, she simply thought about doing those kinds of things. She was self-deprecating and a builder of others. She saw potential *in everyone*. She could talk to strangers, assess their needs, and do anything in her power to bring blessings and good fortune to fruition. She was an advocate for others and would go out on a limb for a total stranger to speak the truth on their behalf. Never was it an act. She was 100 percent genuine. The true "Real Deal." In essence, she cared and was dedicated to living her life making a difference.

So to answer my earlier question, "What did she have that I didn't?" It would unfold over time that the true answer was nothing . . . and everything.

We all possess "C's" magical gift, yet many of us choose not to use it. The trait that this incredible human being had was the knowledge that she was fully human, and she embraced it. In every situation, she was confident enough in herself to authentically bring *all* of herself to the table. And the truth is, she taught me to be comfortable bringing *all of me* too. The *real* me. For the put-together perfectionist that always looked the part, acted the part, and worried constantly about appearances and what others might think, C was a breath of fresh air, one who gave me permission to be me.

C taught me that it was not only okay for people to see the real, imperfect, flawed, quirky, a little weird, beautiful person that I am, but that by being me, I was inviting others to be themselves as well.

When we fully accept ourselves as the unique people we are and stand in our power, we invite others to do the same.

- What would happen if everyone saw you for who you really are?

C was kind to her very core. She was a fearless woman who had a powerful story of her own. A single mom for many years, she was tough. She had to be. She rose through the ranks in politics—living her truth in one of the roughest, male-dominated environments that exist. Her life's purpose was to serve the people who needed her and were counting on her. When I say she stood for the people, it is 100 percent true. One day, for all our sakes, I hope she will be our president. She'd have my vote in an instant.

Of the many lessons she taught, one that has always stayed with me is to speak up for the injustices that you see. She would note, "You *are* the voice. If not you, then who? *Don't* look away." And I listened.

STEP TWO: DO GOOD

Living your truth is risky. It means there's a chance that others might not like you or your viewpoint. It could mean the loss of a job or even lifestyle changes. It could mean the abandonment of some friends if your true thoughts and views were to be made known. If we're truthful, isn't it easier to simply hide away, melding in with the crowd, and not stand out? Yet, C taught me that my silence isn't worth the price. There may be people that you've noticed suffering today that are still waiting for "just one" to stand with them and make a difference, a call for change. Where are hope and justice if you remain silent? Or, as C would say, "If not you, then who?"

C taught me about taking action. She didn't live through words—words can be easy, too convenient. It was her actions that said everything. She lived her life with an absolute refusal to follow the status quo. Standing up for injustice was her solemn vow. She would make a difference, even if it cost her everything. She helped anyone; total strangers learned her name. I've seen C try to get people jobs, listen to their stories and concerns, and do her best to make a difference in their lives. Was it all an act? What was in it for her? The truth is nothing. She is completely authentic and selfless. She didn't know how to think only about herself or her intimate circle. Her life was dedicated to the needs of *many* others.

Each of us has a unique lens for life. A perspective that, like a radar system, goes off when someone or something is "wronged." Yet how often do we silence our warning systems because they sound the alarm when it's not convenient? Sometimes, it's easier to look the other way and pretend we don't see the injustice, isn't it?

C would say, "Find your truth and go speak it. Live your truth." As C often challenged me to ask, I'll ask you: "What are you waiting for?" Time was not an endless commodity for C. For her, the time was always *now*. And it was up to her to lead the way.

- What has God put on your heart to see that others don't see, or pretend not to?
- Whose lives would be better . . .
  1. If only *you* gave them a voice?
  2. If only *you* decided they mattered?
  3. If only *you* cared enough to stand in the gap and speak their truth?

We all have one life to do live. One life to do good. Why not start now? Wouldn't the world be different if all the "good people" showed up?

STEP THREE: BE KIND

In these times, one only has to turn on the news, open an email, or walk down the street to see event after event where people are putting down others to uplift themselves. When did we get to such a point that everyone has it out for those that stand next to them? Whether it's anger and violence that makes the news every evening, the colleague that takes credit for our work and provides unkind remarks, putting us down to make themselves look better, or a family member who wants to battle it out in front of the kids, hate, anger, unkindness, and other emotions like these are growing at epidemic rates. There is a plague spreading across our country, one of preposterous proportions. And countless victims are being harmed.

Ephesians 4:29 says, "Let no corrupting talk come out of your mouths, but only such as is good for building up, as fits the occasion, that it may give grace to those who hear." The lesson C taught was not only to live my truth and do good but equally as impactful was the lesson to be kind in the process.

C was not a "goody-good" person as my sisters might have said. Her kindness was not "for show." She had a true heart of compassion for others. There is an old saying that goes, "Toss a stone in any direction; wherever it lands, that person probably has it much harder than you." I've been humbled by these words as I've learned of the trials others have endured— unimaginable trials even worse than my own. I honestly don't know how some people have gotten through their loss and pain.

The truth is, we never know what a person is going through until we have learned their story or lived in their shoes. And while we often spew our beliefs and thoughts to others, who anxiously await our gossip, innocent people are getting hurt. We are hurting one another.

All too often we are too busy serving our own interests to do the right thing and be kind. I've seen this example play out time and time again, most frequently by women acting out against other women. It's not uncommon for women to neglect to be kind to other women. It seems rare to hear women building each other up. To give another woman a compliment, such as "You look beautiful today!" It's almost unheard of. Women tend to be critical of other women—particularly of women in leadership. *Who do they think they are?* Followed by a host of comments and a gathering of other women to speak against them. I've endured this throughout my life as several women colleagues have been some of my harshest critics.

For the record, men generally don't behave like this. Men usually lift each other up and congratulate each other, often followed by a pat on the back and a beer. I'm not sure if it is ingrained in our DNA or simply the desire to beat another woman out as we compete for attention. Is it an unfilled desire to return to early school days and say, "Who is prettier? And if you think she is, and if she is talented too, then let me knock her down a few pegs."

Regardless of the reason, this kind of attitude isn't serving anyone, and we must stop. The truth is our unkindness is killing us as a collective people, humanity. It's making people miserable, causing them to harm themselves and at times, even ending their lives. Simply put, it is *wrong*.

Certain sayings have been ingrained in our culture, and we can recite them word for word. The Golden Rule is one of these. It comes from the Sermon on the Mount. In Matthew 7:12, the Bible directs us, "So then, in everything treat others the same way you want them to treat you, for this is the essence of the Law and the writings of the Prophets."

Isn't it time we start being kind and treating people as we want to be treated? You've seen on the news the angry and hateful individuals, whose aim is to stir the hearts of fellow citizens, cause violence and unrest in otherwise peaceful neighborhoods. Countless innocent people of all races, genders, and ages have been harmed financially, emotionally, even physically from the hands and words of people meaning to incite violence. Even those in leadership positions often use their power to infuse anger and hate. They speak against "the other side" and stir up friction in hopes of breathing a new, false life and stoking the flames of hate and anger.

Kindness is a choice. Exercised in generous proportions, it brings about good words, thoughts, deeds, and action. Armed with kindness and positive action, we can move generations forward.

As Proverbs 15:14–15 reminds us, "A gentle answer turns away wrath, but a harsh word stirs up anger. The tongue of the wise commends knowledge, but the mouth of the fool gushes folly." And Proverbs 12:18 says, "Thoughtless speech is like the wounds of a sword, but the tongue of the wise is healing."

STEP FOUR: BE THE CHANGE

C taught me many lessons. Her life, with all its choices and deeds, is an inspiration to anyone whom she encounters. What I've learned foremost is that it begins with a life of action. We all have choices and free will. Children learn from the environment in which they are raised about how to treat others, react to situations, and, in many ways, how to behave. Our actions and forward movements make a difference, not only in our lives but the lives of others. Children are always watching and learning.

Sometimes, our true thoughts are apparent in what we say or do. Other times, our actions are more subtle in the way that we treat others, the words that are spoken, and the tone we use. Always though, we show who we are by *how* we live our everyday lives. Are we kind? Do we bully others? Is ours the only voice that needs to be heard? How do we treat others? Do we include others in the conversation or only invite our friends? Do we stand up and speak up for those who can do nothing for us?

Sometimes, it may be our inaction that speaks for us. Not using our voices is sometimes just as strong of a statement to those watching and the world around us. Do we refrain from speaking up? Do we use the influence that we've been given, our power and positions, to advocate for others? Or do we remain silent to be in the "in crowd?"

I believe that Gandhi said it best about how we should live our truth.

An unknown source said, "Be the change you wish to see in the world."

- What is the change that you are being prompted to see?
- How can you live your life to be your 100% authentic self?
- What might living your truth look like for you?

Chapter 7

STAND IN YOUR POWER

"**A**s we prepare for takeoff, please listen to your flight attendants for our safety procedures . . ."

Have you ever wondered why we need to have these instructions stated before every flight? They are a reminder that whether this is your thousandth flight or your very first, you are taking a journey. It is the airline's duty to make sure you are prepared for whatever lies ahead. The road ahead might be smooth, or it may get bumpy—even turbulent—or it may have unseen emergencies. Regardless of the scenario, each of the passengers should be prepared.

Much like a trip via airplane, in this journey called life, God equips us with everything we will need for what lies ahead of us through His instruction book, the

Bible. The Bible talks about God's creation of us in Psalms 139:13–14. "For you created my inmost being; you knit me together in my mother's womb. I praise you because I am fearfully and wonderfully made; your works are wonderful; I know that full well."

God is our Author, our Maker. He alone made us into being. Every part of us—our strong suits, character, strengths, and even our weaknesses—are made perfect in Him. He knows us through and through. As it says in Jeremiah 29:11, "For the plans I have for you, declares the Lord, are plans to prosper you and not to harm you, plans to give you hope and a future."

Not only did He make us for success, but He also gave us a roadmap for the life He wants us to follow. As it says in Psalms 119:105 (KJV), "Thy word is a lamp unto my feet and a light unto my path." The Bible is our guide as He lays out His Story for us to learn and emulate. In times of trouble, it leads us forward and gives us hope. It gives us a bigger perspective and a lens through which to view life, rather than with merely our own thoughts. It constantly reminds us of His bigger plan for us. In John 14:3, it states, "And if I go and prepare a place for you, I will come back and take you to be with me that where I am you may be also." The Bible is our biblical authority for how to live, as it refers to the teachings of God and Jesus. In John 14:6, Jesus says, "I am the way, and the truth, and the life. No one comes to the Father except through me."

Yet, although God made us, equips us, guides us, and gives us our futures, how often do we attempt to go "off-road" on our own journeys instead of the path He intends for us? While the Bible is our instruction book and a guide as it shows us who God is, a caveat it could have on the first page might be: "This is the way to happiness . . . if you'll trust me, learn about me, and listen to my instructions." Instead, we push aside all of His rules and guidelines and say to our living God, "Don't worry God, we've got this!"

STEP ONE: RECOGNIZE THE FOG

"Put on your own oxygen mask first, then you can help others."

Without the proper amount of oxygen, the body can experience confusion, dizziness, rapid breathing, and a racing heart. Without a clear mind, it is easy to get lost, become disoriented, and lose our ways.

I was lost. The toxic environment I was living in with my boss had derailed me and my ability to move forward. A thick fog had settled in, and my visibility was down to nearly nothing. The road ahead was dimly lit. I couldn't see what was ahead. I had an inability to focus. In the midst of the fog, I was disoriented and did not know where I was.

Was this even real, what I was going through? It didn't feel right. Others who I talked to about my current situation—the demands and treatment I was experiencing—couldn't believe the stories. I lived in utter chaos. In my effort to achieve, I was operating under the mode that "doing more" and "trying harder" was the answer. I was failing miserably, and there was no end in sight. I was jumping the high hurdles in my attempt to "make it happen." I could do it, I knew, if I just kept going. This was what I trained for. I was resilient. So I kept plodding forward; it was the only answer.

When we look outside of ourselves for the approval that we're seeking, we will never find it. No amount of love, acceptance, praise, worthiness, permission—whatever it is you are seeking—can be found through others.

Colossians 3:23–24 (ESV) says, "Whatever you do, work heartily, as for the Lord and not for men, knowing that from the Lord you will receive the inheritance as your reward. You are serving the Lord Christ."

Do we actually believe that we are in control of our lives? That somehow, "We've got this?" That if we work hard to achieve, we can make anything happen? In utter transparency, as a self-proclaimed maximizer, I have often been caught up in this misguided truth that yes, somehow, I *am in control*. It's a weakness, I know.

Yet believe me when I say that, thankfully, God has always brought me back to reality and shown me His humble truth. He is in control. Period. (Note, this is not a question.)

It is this fallback operational belief system that purveys its existence when all is completely out of control in my life. It's a reminder: I'd been here before. Though this time, I couldn't identify it. I was lost, alone, and drowning.

In my endless attempts to give it my all, I had lost myself. I was in the thick of the forest and could no longer see the beauty of the trees or even a ray of light. I was working ten-hour days, trying to do all of the "right" things. I couldn't do any more to please this person. I was all but doing backflips and standing on my head in my attempts to try. Nothing would satisfy her. It felt like her primary purpose was to crush me—bury me in task after task. She was reviling in watching me drown.

This was her approach. If she won, then maybe I would finally give up and quit. The weight was heavy, and I was fighting for air to breathe. Why was I still trying to achieve? I was like a workhorse that might work itself into the grave (a.k.a., death), simply to please its master.

Every finished product had been done in excellence so there was nothing to criticize. Unfortunately, no praise was ever given; instead, she added more tasks to my endless list. Near the end, she would meet with me daily to heap more onto the mountain that was that list. Those who witnessed what was happening realized this wasn't right, but nothing changed.

Her position had a name—toxic boss. I was experiencing what many under her had experienced before. She was a bully and was out of control.

Even if not aimed at me, yelling often resonated from the walls of her office. It could be heard from a distance despite her closed door. Whether it was some soul inside that was enduring her wrath or a person on the other end of the phone, it was an ongoing occurrence. There was a long line of the carnage of those who had been beaten and left to cower, as well as a list of those who had gotten away. Her treatment of others was a known elephant in the room, which everyone talked about at the water cooler. "How could a person in her position be allowed to act this way?" everyone asked.

You could either join her or be crushed by her. She had her mignons—good people who became tyrants-in-training. They were once kind people but had been at the crossroads and decided to join her rather than be eaten or crushed. She continued to build her army, recruiting those she could control, inflicting pain on anyone who got in her way.

One day, all of that mattered to me personally. I was the victim who was drowning in her tasks, her brutal words, and her belittling actions. It was her plan. A plan to ruin *me*. A plan to make me feel inadequate, keep me low, and suppress me. Dictators often take stances such as these. They make the people behind them feel less than to keep them down, humiliated, and debilitated so they don't try to gain the dictator's power.

Such were the days of the fog.

STEP TWO: KNOW THYSELF

"Come to me, all you who are weary and burdened, and I will give you rest. Take my yoke upon you and learn from me, for I am gentle and humble in heart, and you will find rest for your souls," reads Matthew 11: 29–30. And I was weary.

I had lost the one thing I had in my life. The one thing I could count on. I had lost my purpose and direction. In that state, I had lost myself. I had allowed one person to make me feel unworthy, to doubt everything about my abilities, talents, and self-worth. I was drowning in her grasp. My world was turned upside down and my soul was dying.

Hitting rock bottom has a way of bringing clarity. It was through my spinning out of control that I fell down on my knees and reached out to the only One

I knew who held the answers. God was my refuge. I was at the end of myself. In my out-of-control state, I was grasping for the One who has always been my constant for answers, my everything. Through the fog, He reminded me of *who I am and Whose I am*.

Never let someone take your power.

When you worship money, power, position, and things, they are empty and will return void. It is easy now to see that in my quest to achieve, to gain power and recognition, I had fallen prey to the traps that come with moving up the ladder of success. My newfound position, the achievement of my six-figure salary, my new title, and my rank—all these things had come at a deadly cost. The intoxication of power, recognition, and fame had created a detour from what is most important in life: a constant relationship with our Lord. God had been put on the back burner with me out front in my quest to do it on my own. I don't believe it was intentional or a conscious thought. It was the trap that too many of us fall into.

We can do it. We're strong. We're able. We've worked so hard to finally get here. All the while, God sits by and allows us to learn this invaluable lesson the hard way because He loves us. The path before me clearly showed that I was holding on too tight. I was grasping for control. I was in charge. I could do it on my own, without anyone's help, including His.

Have you ever had these thoughts? When you're sure that you've got your life under control, yet everything around you seems as if it were underwater? I had achieved my goals. By today's standards, I was a success. Yet my world was collapsing in front of me, and God was patiently waiting to give me a life raft.

There is an Arabic saying that I've applied to the one true God: "*In sha Allah*," meaning, "If God wills it" or "God willing." My parents would always say that in everything, do your best. If you give "your best," you can always be satisfied and look at yourself in the mirror without regret. Even if you fail, if you had tried your best, you were a success because you gave it your all. The lesson here was that try as I might, I couldn't resolve this situation with my boss on my own. I was doing my all, yet God was not willing for me to handle this situation alone. All indications pointed to Him saying to let go and let Him.

Just like Matthew 11:29–30 instructs, "Take my yoke upon you and learn from me, for I am gentle and humble in heart, and you will find rest for your souls."

God *must* be the center of our lives. He allows us to cast Him aside for only a period of time because He allows us free choice. "*In sha Allah*" puts God at the center where He belongs. It begs us to affirm, "If it is

His will, His choice." When God is at the center and we rely on Him, we will find our rest. Our compass and roadmap will lead us forward into what He wants for our lives.

STEP THREE: "TO THINE OWN SELF BE TRUE" (William Shakespeare)

While in the fog, it's hard to see what is before you. Much like with a lack of oxygen, we can easily become disoriented. Even the most familiar of roads and places can often appear to be foreign lands.

Have you ever noticed after the fog has lifted, how bright and clear the path ahead becomes? It sometimes takes our eyes time to adjust to the light and clarity. It is a relief. We can breathe deep again and forge ahead confidently.

This is much like what having Jesus in our lives does for our paths. We are made in His own image, with all the qualities, traits, instincts, beliefs, and determination He created inside us. If we stay close to Him, we will thrive. Life is easier. The path ahead is clearer, and we can rest in Him. As we drift or depart from Him, our worlds fall apart.

We were made to be His. Shakespeare said it best when he wrote, "This above all, to thine own self be true." When we allow God to truly dwell inside us, our compass is assured, and we can count on Him to guide our lives as He designed them. It is when we ignore His life instructions, don't listen, and tune Him out, that we get misguided and can become lost and disoriented.

Whether it is our first time or our thousandth, God's instructions for our lives are worthy to be heard, listened to, and followed. Taking time to listen and hear His daily instructions will lead to immeasurable joy and a life worthy of being called His.

STEP FOUR: STAND IN YOUR POWER

"Jesus said to the Jews who had believed him, 'If you abide in my word, you are truly my disciples, and you will know the truth, and the truth will set you free'" (John 8:31–32). Life with Jesus at the helm ensures our path is headed in the right direction. In Matthew 11:30, Jesus says, "For my yoke is easy, and my burden is light." As humans, we have an innate need and drive to succeed. Abraham Maslow recognized this and authored Maslow's Hierarchy of Needs, which consists of the five levels toward "Self-Actualization." Whether our goal is to achieve wealth, status, recognition, power, love, or belonging—whatever our end goal—God asks us to put Him first. He says in Matthew 6:33, "Seek first the kingdom of God and all things will be added to you."

God beckons us to invite Him into our hopes and dreams: to put Him at the helm and everything else will be added. When we surrender our dreams to God's timing and God's will, we put Him in the driver's seat and allow Him to work in our lives.

Knowing who you are and Whose you are is vital to discovering your true success in this life. When we realize that God is our first parent, the One who knit us together and gave us our every attribute, we understand that He knows the true vision for our lives and He calls them good and perfect. "For I know the plans I have for you," declares the Lord, "plans to prosper you and not to harm you, plans to give you hope and a future" (Jeremiah 29:11).

When we lose sight of God's calling for our lives, we lose all perspective of His desires for our lives to have meaning and purpose for those around us—and ourselves. In reality, God has put in each of us a moral compass. This "inner directional" is strong. Even a toddler innately knows when they are testing the limits and doing something bad. Knowing who you are will allow you to set healthy boundaries around every situation that you encounter.

When I was in "the fog," I realized that my drive to succeed overrode my desire to please God. I was trying to prove myself. With fervor, I wanted to achieve a certain level of success, wealth, recognition, and status. Today, I'm thankful that "the fog" woke me up. I realize today that all of these idols are empty without Him. "Yet indeed I also count all things loss for the excellence of the knowledge of Christ Jesus my Lord, for whom I have suffered the loss of all things, and count them as rubbish, that I may gain Christ" (Philippians 3:8, NKJV).

Living a life filled with integrity, standing for what is right, and letting go of things that clearly are not: that's the goal. As Romans 8:16 states, "For I consider that the sufferings of our present time are not worth comparing with the glory that is to be revealed to us."

When the fog had finally lifted, in the clear of day, I realized that my wants, desires, and boundaries had all been blurred. I regained a clear focus and reset healthy boundaries. Knowing who you are, how you should be treated, and what you bring to every situation is important. Armed with this understanding, I was prepared to draw and maintain healthy boundaries. Boundaries are important in life. They are those "inner-guardrails" that maintain order, guiding us along the way, telling us when danger is ahead or approaching, and directing us on our paths.

Stand in your power is what Polonius was saying in Shakespeare's play, *Hamlet*, when he said, "To thine own self be true." Know your truth. For truly, only the truth will set you free.

Make a list of your qualities, traits, talents, and beliefs. This list is who God created you to be. In the fog, this list is your life raft to hold onto.

- Are there toxic people that have you in a fog? If so, how can you stand tall in your power? How can you silence their voices to hear God's calling in your life?
- Do you need to let go and let God? I have learned the beauty of "*In sha Allah*," or "If God wills it." Might you need this reminder?
- What specifically do you need to let go of today that you are hanging onto too tightly?

Praying "*In sha Allah*," or "If God wills it," (knowing we're praying to the one true God) will put God in charge. Humbling ourselves and submitting our wills to the will of God in our lives allows us to lean into God's purpose for our lives. It's an exciting journey that will take you to places you would have never dreamed of.

Chapter 8

INFLUENCE AND INTEGRITY

*"Having influence is not about elevating self
but about lifting others."*
Sheri Dew

D istinguished, revered, a true professional, and a man of the people. When I met him, it was difficult not to be awestruck. He was a man that many admired. Everywhere we went, people would stop him and want to shake his hand and get a photo with him, simply to be close to him. It was an honor just to say hello. He was a person who had earned the respect of countless others throughout his highly decorated career. A consummate professional, he put the needs of others before his own time after time. People looked up to him. As I stood beside him, I felt a sense of pride and privilege.

Yet even the best is merely human.

STEP ONE: UNDERSTAND THE POWER OF BEING "THE ONE"

Stresses, fear of the unknown, and uncertainty can cause even the most revered leader to falter. There are always crossroads. They encompass decisions to either stand up against popular opinion or give way to pressures and look the other way. When a person has the power to influence for the betterment of others yet chooses to remain silent, it is a tragedy for all.

How often have you wished that someone "in charge" would speak up on your behalf or for others, yet they chose to remain silent? Excuses unfold: "It wasn't the right time" or "We didn't have the support we needed." Unfortunately, many can relate to this scenario as they have lived it themselves. Why is it that when we are finally in the position to influence others, we often take the road less traveled and succumb to going along with the multitudes and choosing not to speak up? We don't want to be the outlier. We wouldn't want anyone to think badly of us. We fret and ask, *What if I'm the only one?*

I experienced this firsthand while working in a prominent role in a job that I loved. The only problem was that it was a highly toxic work environment caused by one. I had an enviable position, a role that others would fight for. People would see our name up in lights and were in awe. "What a great place," I often heard, followed by "You're doing such great things." It is humorous that, in today's world, a flashy marketing campaign, carefully worded slogans, and a noteworthy mission can blind the multitudes. The fault wasn't with the organization. It was with the people who claimed to care. Leaders who misused their power and influence for their gain and who mistreated those within their grasp. Behind the curtain of this organization was a far different view than what people saw from the outside.

A tyrant was allowed to rule, and everyone close to the center knew it. Workers would hear the yelling coming from within the walls; awkward glances would follow, and then came the eye-rolls, as if saying, "We've heard this before." On occasion, one might have uttered a soft comment under one's breath before they quickly moved on. How such a person could rise to the top with such unprofessionalism and horrible treatment toward others is a mystery; yet it happens every day in corporate America, within a myriad of companies. Everyone knows it.

In our case, management allowed it to happen, choosing to either defend the behavior or look the other way. Other leaders who showed integrity, professionalism, and talent were overlooked. This person ruled, and if you dared to go up against them, you, too, might suddenly vanish.

Yet this distinguished man who was revered by the multitudes . . . surely, he would stand up and call this person out, right? After all, he was the picture of integrity with a history filled with making all the right choices. If someone was able to do something, it would be him. He now had the power. Yet the reality, what was more tragic than the behavior of the tyrant; it was the deafening silence that followed after telling him his defense was needed.

For all my high praise and accolades, I was utterly dismayed when it came time for me to take a stand for what was right, and he retreated and looked the other way.

When a person of influence has the opportunity to change something and knowingly chooses to look the other way, it is unfortunate for all involved. Leaders have a responsibility to come to the aid of others and defend what is right. This responsibility sits in the definition of leadership. According to MindTools, "Leaders help themselves and others to do the right things. They set direction, build an inspiring vision, and create something new. Leadership is about mapping out where you need to go to 'win' as a team or an organization; and it is dynamic, exciting, and inspiring."[1]

Leadership is not easy. To stand up for what is right and speak up, requires one to be brave. Leadership involves action to swim against the stream and be a voice for the voiceless. These acts themselves put one at a higher risk of being isolated, alone, and opening ourselves up to personal criticism.

- Is it our selfish nature to want to look good, to be deemed important and admired at any cost?
- What would you do or say to have the praise of others?
- Would you stand up against the pack to be "the one" for others?

For this chairperson, standing up against the pack would have come at too high of a cost. It could mean the healthy paycheck disappears, the nice title, the position of power and importance that made it too difficult to risk losing. One person's disappointment wasn't worth the possibility of losing social status and lifestyle. And with that action, other leaders who also knew the truth followed suit. It was easier to remain silent than to be

1   "What is Leadership?" MindTools, accessed 9 Dec 2021, https://www.mindtools.com/pages/article/newLDR_41.htm.

singled out and ostracized. After all, they would say, who was I to speak up? They feared losing prestige, perks, and the identity that went with their roles and within their elite circles. It was easier to pretend everything was good and look the other way.

A wise woman, my mom, often told me, "Two wrongs don't make a right." Moms are revered for their wisdom and truth. This saying is another example of this. My mom taught me: "Do what is right." This is how I learned about integrity.

STEP TWO: BE WILLING TO STAND ALONE

Integrity, as defined online by Oxford Languages, is, "the quality of being honest and having strong moral principles; moral uprightness." Other descriptions include, "doing the right thing in a reliable way; a person who has a moral compass that doesn't waver; a wholeness of character."

What does it take to live a life in which you're willing to stand up for what is right? There are positions where people are absolutely expected to operate with integrity. Priests and other clergy members, anyone in ministry, would rank high on this list. One might say, anyone who is committed to public service and the common good of others would surely have such characteristics. Yet all humans are flawed and capable of being "less than our best selves" in different circumstances.

I was once asked to take a position with an organization by the leader of that organization. He just so happened to also be a prominent member of our community. Instantly, I *knew* I could trust him and the offer. There wasn't time to draft a contract. I jumped in with both feet to help out in a difficult circumstance. "Of course, I'll begin work. We can work out the details later."

We had already worked out things like pay, hours, and expectations. I felt good about the reasonable amount I would be paid for the job that I was being asked to do. I was all set, or so I thought. Until he told me he made a mistake. The finance person thought there was an error with his math. They believed he had agreed to pay me too much. He couldn't tell the others involved about our agreement. It was a "misunderstanding," he told me, "between us." Yes, we did have an agreement. However, confessing it to the other board members who might think it was too much would make him look bad.

Fast forward, and I was quickly replaced by a peer, who generously offered to work in the role at a lower rate. Even people who we expect to act with integrity can disappoint us at times. We are all human. Again, I turned to my mom's wisdom as her words spoke to my soul, "Do not look to people. People may disappoint you. Turn your eyes to Heaven and look to God. He will never disappoint you."

Integrity involves telling the truth at all costs. It is owning up to our mistakes and not making excuses for them. Influence and integrity go hand-in-hand. When we are put in positions of leadership, we are expected to act with integrity and do the right thing. Leaders have the responsibility to lead even when it comes at great personal risk. Leadership is a privilege. It involves taking care of others before yourself, even to your detriment. It isn't about the title, the money, or the perks.

There have been countless people throughout my life who I have looked up to for the influence they have had on my life, and even more so for the integrity in which they operated. I hope you have started your list too. These are people that we all esteem to be more like.

"Integrity," as C.S. Lewis once stated, "is doing the right thing, even when no one is watching." "Integrity is choosing your actions based on values rather than personal gain."

- Who has been "the one" for you?
- Are you willing to stand alone for others? If not, why not?
- What holds you back from operating with integrity? Is this something you can work on?
- Who can you be "the one" for?

This chapter is dedicated to three beautiful souls who have modeled integrity and who my life has been truly blessed by knowing: Mike Howland, Theresa Petrarca, and John Qualls.

Chapter 9

BEWARE OF THE FAKERS

We all know them. People that "lead" by using their power. They leave a path of destruction, one littered with anything that got in their way. They are out for themselves and their best interests. This is a category of people I refer to as the "fakers."

We often find these people in positions of leadership, as they thrive on ruling over others. They disguise themselves as leaders, but the reality is, they do not resemble anything in the definition of a true leader. It is likely that you have encountered them. Many have experienced firsthand the destruction they can cause. These are people who take credit for the work of others and use every opportunity to push down those under their sphere of power and influence to exalt themselves.

Yet, there is a bright side. If we allow it, these individuals can serve as the motivators to push us further, to achieve greater heights despite them and their actions.

The power of fakers is their ability to intimidate. They rule through the use of fear, threats, yelling, harassment, and demeaning behaviors. One might ask, "When did these bad behaviors become acceptable in our business world? When did we start heralding those who act deplorable and give them the title of *leader*?" These are tough questions that must be asked. We need to begin holding those in charge accountable for their actions and their directions as future generations are looking to them and their behaviors for guidance. We must begin discerning character, in addition to skillset and talents, as a threshold for attaining leadership status.

Fakers are all around us, found every day in small, mid-sized, and large companies. These types of people roam every sector of business and government, public and private office, and even at the highest-ranking positions. These people have power and influence, yet their modes of operation include having low integrity, selfishness, corruption, and participating in evil doings. Innocent people suffer every day at the hands of these intimidators. Hard-working people cower and look aside at the actions of these tyrants as they sheepishly and dutifully do their jobs, effectively lifting these fakers up because of their titles and ranking positions. Even those higher up the ranks recognize these tyrants. They know the truth yet excuse their behavior, choosing instead not to deal with them. After all, it's an easier path with less confrontation.

Fakers do not act alone. They are, at their core, insecure people who grapple for power. Without others, they have no one to have power over. They look for the weak and the meek, people whom they can control. They ban together with them and lift these people to power with them, as they build loyalty, trust, and a following. They are aware there is power in numbers. Together, they rule by forming a formidable team to badger, intimidate, and outnumber those around them. Tyrants, with their armies all around them, take control and will take down anyone or anything that threatens their way.

We all know fakers. But how can we live, co-exist, and even thrive in their world? There are three important steps to bringing victory. Each of these important steps has a single, unifying element at its core: the ability to understand, create, and set strong boundaries.

STEP ONE: CUT THE NOISE

According to Wikipedia, "Personal boundaries are guidelines, rules or limits that a person creates to identify reasonable, safe and permissible ways for other people to behave towards them and how they will respond when someone passes those limits."

As a self-proclaimed boundary-less person, I didn't learn what boundaries were until later in life. I didn't understand the concept. You mean, a person has a choice of how they will be treated by others? It was a foreign concept that, somehow, I had missed during my upbringing. I had to learn this lesson on the flip-side. I am a survivor. I've experienced a highly toxic and abusive relationship that was meant to destroy me but instead, taught me about boundaries.

It is important to note that boundaries have two parts: 1) They are behaviors we deem acceptable or unacceptable by others, and they bring about 2) rules of conduct of how we allow ourselves to respond once these behaviors are kept or broken.

The first step in learning how to co-exist with fakers is to cut the noise. This involves knowing yourself. We must know who we are at the core of our being because fakers will push you to your core, poke and make fun of it, and even discount it with every chance they get. One of their modes of operation is to inflict self-doubt. To have you question who you are is their first step in chipping away at the foundation of your being. They want to define you; it is a part of how they gain control. So, it is *vital* that you know who you are. By defining yourself and knowing who you are and who you are not, they will not be able to crack your foundation. Remember:

"To thine own self be true."
Shakespeare

Write down on a piece of paper the things you love about yourself. Start with the statement, "I am . . ." Really dig deep.

- What are the things that make you uniquely you?
- Are you fun?
- Are you playful?
- Do you challenge the status quo?

Have fun with this. It's your time to celebrate *you*!

- What are the things you most admire about yourself?
- What are you most proud of that you've accomplished?

Knowing yourself is vital to your ability to stand tall and firm in your power.

This simple act of writing your list is the first step of you taking back your power from these people who are bent on taking it away. So when the faker is telling you all the things that you know are not the truth, you can cut the noise. They are just words.

"Just because words are said
does not mean they are the truth."
Mom

My mom—such a wise woman! Wisdom is developed through experiences. Usually, it comes through a cost. I am thankful that my mom spoke these words into my soul: "Just because they say the words, it does not make them true." In that statement, my mom gave me the wisdom of and approval to use discernment. I give you this same permission. Never let someone else define who you are.

Fakers try to wear down their opponents with lies. Fakers do not want to be your friends. They are out to either silence you, control you, or have you come over to their side. They are not middle-of-the-road, neutral people. You knowing who you are is vital to coexisting in a faker's world.

STEP TWO: STAND TALL AND STAND FIRM

Fakers have weaknesses. Fakers are insecure and jealous people. Though, they come across as just the opposite. They appear confident, even arrogant about who they are. They want to have your admiration—your "awe" of them. They want to be looked up to and respected, have people cater to their needs. So if you are not going to "join them," you must be able to stand your ground.

Fakers are easily intimidated. At the heart of a faker is a bully. Please read that again. *At the heart of a faker is a bully.* They know if they weren't to bully others and push for their way, people might just see them for who they really are. Often, they are not extraordinarily talented. They are ruthless, relentless, insecure people who use others' talents to climb their way to the top and earn titles to hide behind. Bullies act the way they do because they are constantly in fear of being found out.

Their behavior continues because few individuals have the courage to stand up to them. The vast majority of people will not risk it all to call them out on their deplorable actions. Most people either look the other way, move on to other positions, or join their team. To the person who stands tall and firm, looks them in the eye, and affirms who they are—and that what the faker is doing is wrong—it may mean the end of a career or other serious repercussions. Therefore, knowing who you are at your core will help you speak truth into your situation.

I once was told by someone older, who was in a position of power, that I needed to just "go along to get along." To a person with high integrity and self-worth, this statement was a challenge. I learned that it is not genuine or worthy advice.

*"While standing tall and firm has
the potential to come at high personal risk,
the greater risk is losing yourself."*
J.L. Dedon

To expand: While standing tall and firm has the potential to come at high personal risk, the greater risk is losing yourself, your health, and your mental well-being to a faker who would love to take your worth away. What is your price for authenticity?

For me, the loss that came did not compare to having the strength to stand tall and firm with my convictions and truth in hand, to stand up against the giant. While I did end up walking away, I left on my terms and told the truth. With my head held high, I lived my truth, stayed true to my convictions, and the chains were broken. I was free. "And the truth shall set you free" (John 8:31–32).

STEP THREE: CREATE A POSITIVE IMPACT

My people matter. Bondage no more. These were the words I heard over and over. It took knowing who I am, setting firm boundaries, telling my truth, standing tall and firm, and being willing to walk out the door with my head held high to finally be free. How about you? I felt every bit of this: "To bestow on them a crown of beauty instead of ashes" (Isaiah 61:1–3).

What is the positive impact that the world is waiting on you to make? What is your story that needs to be told? Had it not been for living through the circumstances of my life—which at times brought me to the end of myself, forced me to stand, and voice my truth—this book would never have been written. Truly, we have an amazing God who brings beauty from ashes.

Each of us has but one life to live. Our responsibility in this life is to make the world better for others. To create a positive impact wherever we go and whatever we do. Cowering in my silence would have kept me in my position; it would have continued to bring home a nice paycheck for a longer duration, and I would have kept the nice title. Yet how many lives, including my own, would have paid the price? It takes *one* to lead. It takes one to say, "No more." It takes one to say, "This is wrong and will not continue." To call out injustices and forge a new path. One. It is not the multitude that makes the first step toward difference. The multitudes change the course of time, yes. But it begins with the one. May God grant you the passion of your convictions, the strength to believe, and the courage to stand tall and firm to create a positive impact for the many who are waiting for you.

"Never let someone silence your voice."
J.L. Dedon

My people matter. Bondage no more.

- What wrongs are you seeing that need to be given a voice?
- What is it that is gnawing at you that you can't let go of?
- Is someone telling you that you are "less than"?
- Is it time that you take back your power and stand tall and stand firm?
- Who can you be "the one" for?

This chapter is dedicated to the fakers who underscore who we are to bring us to the point of being Silent No More.

Chapter 10

BE SILENT NO MORE

You were created for a purpose. Everything that has happened to you up to this point in your life has happened as a part of your story. Do you know that? Everything. The good, the bad, even the ugliest parts all have meaning for you to give voice to. Did you know that your voice could be a difference in someone else's life? You could be the answer to a prayer that someone is praying right now.

God has been whispering into my soul for a long time. Since childhood, I have felt His presence. I've always known He is here. As a little girl in a church pew standing up and giving my testimony among the adults, I yearned to be closer to Him. I couldn't hold back singing His praises in my life.

Fast forward to the time when I was on my knees rocking back and forth as the anxiety that consumed my body overwhelmed me. I was overridden with that anxiety and experiencing post-traumatic stress. My world was unknown, foreign. Every moment was painful. It is traumatic to feel like a foreigner inside your own body. To feel trapped inside an outward shell. Yet I was aware of who I was, and I wanted "normalcy" back. I wanted to wake up and feel like me again. I wanted my life back.

As I rocked back and forth, a stress-relieving exercise my therapist had suggested, I felt a touch on my back. I know, it sounds crazy. There was no one in the room. But it was real. It was an angel, I suspect. I definitely felt it. For a split moment, I wondered, could this be? And then I knew. My loving God, in my absolute despair, was there. With me, comforting me. I will never forget that day. In my dark hole, He found me. He did not forget me. He came with me and was beside me. His hand said, I am with you, and you are not alone. I know that I could have given up that night. It was not a way to live, and there was too much pain. I wondered if I would ever be the same or normal again. Would I ever be able to feel like me again? Why is this happening? So many thoughts raced through my head. I could not quiet the whirlwind in my mind, the constant shaking of my body. My arms, hands, and legs

. . . they all exposed my trembling condition. It was noticeable, even to others. I could not hide. Yet in my lowest moment, He was there with me.

How could I, someone so insignificant, matter to the One, the Almighty, our Omnipotent Lord and Savior? The answer: His promise is for real. You can count on it. He does not disappoint. *Ever.* For as Matthew 10:29–31 says, "Are not two sparrows sold for a penny? And not one of them will fall to the ground apart from the Father . . . Fear not, therefore; you are of more value than many sparrows." And "Therefore, I tell you, do not be anxious about your life, what you will eat or what you will drink, nor about your body, what you will put on . . . Consider the lilies of the field, how they grow: they neither toil nor spin, yet I tell you, even Solomon in all his glory was not arrayed like one of these" (Matthew 6:25 and 34). Finally, John 3:16 says, "For God so loved the world that He gave His one and only Son, that whoever believes in Him shall not perish but have eternal life."

Over and over again I have survived the depths of despair and stood on the mountain tops. He has given me the courage to stand. To fight through every circumstance. To get up every time I've been knocked down. Every step, every trial, every moment, He has been there. The victory is His. Leading up and throughout my life, He has been weaving a beautiful tapestry.

Through the times when I felt all alone with shattered glass all around me, when I could not move, I sat, picking up the pieces of my life one by one, always with His help. Picking up the pieces that He then helped me put together—until there was no more glass, and a beautiful, stunning image appeared. I am strong, whole, confident; I have survived.

The events that inspired this book form the tapestry of my life. He built me into who I am today. He made me, like you, in His image and for a purpose. I have heard His whispers in my soul. He is there. "My people matter." Yes, I matter and so do you.

> **And we know that for those who love God**
> **all things work together for good, for those**
> **who are called according to His purpose.**
> **Romans 8:28**

STEP ONE: TAKE BABY STEPS

It was by far the hardest day of my life. Harder than my sudden divorce, the death of a parent, or the general shockwaves and difficulties that come throughout life. Post-traumatic stress symptoms. They are real and what I had been experiencing finally had a name. When your mind holds your body captive to the point you don't recognize yourself, it strips you of all trust in yourself and in others. It takes away all confidence and makes you question everything. This can happen when the mind goes through too much trauma and begins shutting itself down to protect itself.

Looking back on that day is still painful. I can still feel, smell, and hear everything about that day The years have passed, and the acute pain of that time has faded; however, the brain does not forget what it has endured. I remember breathing through every minute and wanting to give up. "Just take baby steps," my mom said. "Try to get through the next five minutes and call me back." Every minute seemed like an eternity. Each minute passed slowly while my body was nerve-wracked, shaking, and my mind raced. "Baby steps" her soft voice whispered gently, yet with authority and trust.

Baby steps and my beautiful mom saved my life. Throughout the years, I have said these same words to bring encouragement to countless people who were at that same turning point. "Just take baby steps." I've gotten the weird looks and glances that come with that advice. But for all the souls that need to hear these words, I've learned to trust that "baby steps" are exactly what is needed sometimes.

Human babies are born without the ability to walk. They are carried. They learn to walk over time. God placed within each of us a desire to want to be independent and strong. Yet sometimes, depending on what we've endured, we need to crawl or take baby steps again. We do not possess the strength to walk on our own, so we revert to foundational movements. We get to start over.

Years later, I would say these same words back to my mom after she went through double-knee replacement surgery. She wanted to give up; the pain was too unbearable. I understood. "Keep going, Mom. Just take baby steps." Then years later when she suffered from debilitating spine pain. "Just take baby steps," I would say to her. "One step at a time, Mom."

I don't know why we have to endure the pain that we go through. But I do know that without the pain, without the trials, we would not be the people that we are to become. It is through these trials and circumstances that we are molded and shaped, crafted into the magnificent creations that we were designed to be from the beginning.

For all who are experiencing trials, who want it all to go away *right now*, I understand. I, too, wish for the pain and problems to disappear instantly. To be able to snap my fingers and make it happen. My mom would say, "It's going to be all right." Through everything, this was her response. "It's going to be all right." I remember after her passing, my youngest sister said to me, "It isn't all right. It's *not* going to be all right." Why did she say this? I believe my mom knew the truth. As a devoutly religious Christian, my mom was able to set aside self and find solace through the joy of knowing the Lord. She exemplified her name: Joy. She brought joy to all who knew her. I believe she understood that no matter the circumstances around you, He was there in the midst. No matter the pain we experience, or the trials that surround our lives, God is at the helm. She *knew* this. She trusted it 100 percent. And with this truth, everything will be all right in the end. No matter what. As it says in Romans 8:31, "If God is for us, who can ever be against us?" No matter what your circumstance, the Most Holy is with you and goes with you. *It's going to be all right.*

You were created for a purpose. Know that; drink that in. As it says in Psalm 139:13–14, "For you created my inmost being; you knit me together in my mother's womb. I praise you because I am fearfully and wonderfully made." How many of us doubt this? Criticizing ourselves for how we look, for the talents or lack of talents we possess? Many people go through life never finding their mission or why they exist. They doubt His words and His promises. Life is found on the other side of intention.

As shared in "When Your Relationships Are Good, Your Life is Good," a blog entry by Jo-Ann Downey, "Intention is a goal, or vision, that guides your activities, thoughts, attitudes, and choices. Hence your intentions influence your actual experiences."[2] What is it that you want to dedicate your life to doing? What is important to you? First, set your intentions. With clear intentions in mind and living according to your personal values and God at the helm, He will help you achieve and find your life's purpose. It begins with trusting Him. "Let go and let God."

"Leap and the net will appear."
John Burroughs

My dream for writing this book was first and foremost to give God the glory for all that He has done. To speak to "the one" who needed to hear these words and empower you to trust Him and keep going. As a personal cheerleader for others, my primary goal is to help you unlock the *true you* that is waiting to come out. The song "Bless the Broken Road" by Rascal Flatts says it well. Go take a listen.

Throughout the research and writing of this book, I've talked with countless people barred from living their best lives because they are holding themselves back with one phrase, "If only . . ."

- I would be a (fill in the blank), if only . . .

---

2   https://beallofyoutoday.com/

- I want to find another job, if only . . .
- I always wanted to be a (fill in the blank), if only . . .

Isn't it time to seize the day and walk into your destiny?

STEP TWO: GRAB YOUR CAPE

I always wanted to be a superhero. You know, someone with superpowers to save the day. I haven't yet decided which superpowers I would ask for. Perhaps, the ability to heal the sick? The power to read minds? Or the power to fly and have the strength to rescue people from burning buildings, keep a building from falling, or save planes from crashing. Or maybe it would be to save children and adults, dogs, and puppies from being abused. Or to speak out against the injustices I see and beg us all to love and accept one another. What superpowers would you want to possess if you could choose?

What if today you had the power to change your future by making one decision? Where would you start? What is one of the biggest dreams you have for your life? And what is one step you could take *today* to start yourself on that journey? For many, the question to ask is: what if money or time were of no object, what would you do then? It all starts with baby steps.

For me, it was simply the decision to follow him years ago. You might say, "Really? That's it?" It is. I remember looking up at the stars in my backyard and talking to God, saying, "Surely there is more to life than this?" Working, eating, sleeping; it all seemed insignificant. The Maker and Ruler of this earth had to have meant us for more. Then came a point in my life when I realized I had been living for me and what I wanted, not what He wanted for me. It was at that moment that I dedicated my life to serving Him. After all, at that point I found myself, I had made a mess of my life. I was divorced and single with a child who needed me. I simply decided to let go and let God take the lead. At that moment, my prayer began, "Use me . . . .for your glory. Not my will, but your will be done."

Living a life of passion serving Him changed my life. I stopped focusing on myself and what I wanted, striving for what life was going to bring to me. Instead, I was focused on a much larger goal: how could I make a difference in others' lives by serving? What I didn't recognize then was that this decision was a defining moment in my life. At this moment and with that question, I would change the trajectory of my life.

The rewards of this life cannot be measured in dollars or with our bank accounts. God does not value one's net worth in dollars earned. That was a hard and painful lesson to learn. God would instead lead me on a path that would involve working long hours and being underpaid yet flowing over with a passion for others by bringing myself to make and be a difference in their lives. Committing my life to Him meant a life of being His servant and following Him, to be His hands and feet where He needed me. It has been a life of adventure. I have done things I would have never dreamed of (including writing this book). I laid down my life to follow Him and found the joy and abundance to live the life that He imagined for me. I have lived an empowered life. How about you?

You have the power to live the life you have always wanted to as well. It is within your reach. Have you had any defining moments that have guided you on your journey? What are the obstacles to starting your journey? If money or time is an obstacle, try beginning with volunteering or serving others in that area first. Tell others of your dreams and let them help you. Letting go of how you think your life should look and letting Him guide you to your life are two very different approaches. Let go and let God and, I would add, enjoy the journey. Through faith, trust Him to use you for His glory.

STEP THREE: BELIEVE

What would you attempt to do if you knew you would not fail?

Living in the trueness of who you were created to be unlocks the true potential inside of you. Life is a journey, and it begins with you believing you can do it. Finally give yourself permission to fly, even to soar, and go for your dreams. Believing encompasses facing your fears, accepting all of yourself with open arms, and loving yourself—every part of you—as He does. No matter what you've done, despite all of your successes and your failures—ALL OF THEM—He loves you and wants to set you free. Claim your legacy and the impact you will make on your life for others. Armed with your true self, begin by standing firm in your power. Know who you are, and more importantly, Whose you are. Use your influence for good. Be aware that there are champions and fakers out there. Even fakers can help us grow. Learn from them. Learn how *not* to treat people. Learn to stand tall and stand firm and not to give away your power.

When we accept ourselves in the fullest manner, we are able to share our full selves with others and bring impact to others.

When we truly love and accept ourselves, we are able to accept every part of us, and in so doing, we allow our souls to be free from all restraints. When we do this, we then extend this generosity to others and are able to fully accept the wholeness of others. This is our journey to being set free.

Live in the fullness of who you were created to be. Then, and only then, will you be *Silent No More*.

- What is holding you back today?
- Where do you need to take baby steps?
- Where do you want to use your superhero powers to claim your life's work?
- Who is waiting for you to make a difference?
- What would you attempt to do if you knew you could not fail?
- What will it take to be set free and be *Silent No More*?

Chapter 11

TOLERANCE

"But seek first the Kingdom of God and His righteousness
and all these things will be given unto you."
Matthew 6:33

Every generation can learn lessons from one another. As one generation looks to another, we need to do so with a lens toward understanding. Older generations should admire young people, seeing their dreams, their pursuits, and their tenacity as hope for the future. Older generations can champion their minds, their innovations, and new perspectives. Younger generations have so much to learn from the wisdom of older generations. They should admire and respect them, value their viewpoints, and glean the knowledge they have earned and acquired. The wisdom that our elders often share so freely can profoundly impact our lives if we allow it.

Wisdom is defined online by Oxford Languages as, "The quality of having experience, knowledge, and good judgment; the quality of being wise."

King Solomon was said to be the wisest man to have ever lived. Of all the gifts that Solomon could have asked for—money, wealth, or fame—he chose wisdom. [3]

First Kings 4:29–31 shares about Solomon. "God gave Solomon wisdom and very great insight, and a breadth of understanding as measureless as the sand on the seashore. Solomon's wisdom was greater than the wisdom of all the people of the East, and greater than all the wisdom of Egypt. He was wiser than anyone else." Yet if you go on to read the remainder of the chapter, one realizes that Solomon gained wealth, power, influence, and love *and* was miserable. It was at the end of his life that he shared his final piece of wisdom, almost begging each of us not to follow in his footsteps.

"Now all has been heard; here is the conclusion of the matter: Fear God and keep His commandments, for

---

3   Summarized excerpts taken from a blog post titled, "Wisdom from King Solomon at the End of His Life" by Jeff Simmons on March 9, 2017, https://jeffsimmons.org/2017/03/09/wisdom-from-king-solomon-at-the-end-of-his-life/.

this is the whole duty of man. For God will bring every deed into judgment, including every hidden thing, whether it is good or evil" (Ecclesiastes 12: 13–14). Solomon learned that without God, life is meaningless.

Why are wisdom and learning amongst generations so undervalued today? Younger generations brush off the advice and wise counsel of their elders. After all, what do they know? The generalized view is that the elderly are old and antiquated. *I can do better* is the prevailing opinion. Even the elderly often look at the young with irritation, disgust, and dismay. *If only they would listen.* They are "headstrong" I have heard said.

I have found that the older I get, the more I realize that many lessons can be learned by simply stopping to be present and observing. Seek to understand, as there truly is no substitute for wisdom. Wisdom is the one commodity we cannot earn or buy. It comes over time and is earned through experience. It cannot be hastily given. It grows in value through the years as perspectives on life change. The values, goals, and ideals of what you believe in your twenties will drastically change through maturity and life experiences. In your forties and fifties, you learn the follies of the beliefs of your youth. Life's experiences shape and mold us into the people we become. As you learn, you grow and your lens on life will change. Embrace it. There is beauty found in every age.

True beauty, as my mom always told me, is found within. As people age, true beauty really does shine through. Begin to notice older people. Their faces, their demeanor, the way they carry themselves reveal a great amount. People can see what is within a person, beginning with the look on their face. How do they hold themselves? Are they open and welcoming or closed-off and rigid? People will either be attracted to you, or your body language will be closed off, like a guard's gate that keeps people at bay.

So what do wisdom and perspective have to do with tolerance? How we view the world begins with how we view ourselves.

"The eyes are the window to your soul."
William Shakespeare

A person who is optimistic, encouraging, loving, kind, and generous internalizes this viewpoint. Their view of the world is fueled by their thinking and processing of the events that happen to them. These incoming messages are then translated through a lens of optimism, love, and kindness, which in turn shines back on others they encounter.

On the other hand, when a person is fueled by hatred, the judgment of others, and a desire to harm others, their incoming messages are filtered through a lens of hate, criticism, and a desire to inflict harm through words and actions. Any event that happens to them is filtered through this lens and the output is entirely different.

The same incident, happening to both of these types of people, will bring about two distinctly different outcomes. Our perspective and what we bring to a situation play a significant role in determining our outcome.

· What perceptions and beliefs are driving your thoughts today?
· Are your thoughts true to the desired outcome that you are trying to accomplish? Or could there be another way to look at the situation?
· How can your thinking be changed to bring about a new and different outcome?

We all believe our truth is real. If I made a statement that is meant as positive and good, and it is taken in a completely different way, does that make me wrong? Does it mean my intentions were wrong? Or is it the person's fault that they perceived my statement in a completely different way? They misunderstood completely what I said. It all begins with understanding.

STEP ONE: MAKE IT A YEAR OF UNDERSTANDING

After we settled into married life, the youthful bliss of our awestruck opinions of one another began to unravel. Life is real when you begin to share daily life with another person. Hairline cracks in our foundation began to form. How could this person who was perfect for me, who once thought exactly as I thought, who wanted everything that I wanted, suddenly be so different from me? If you have been married for any amount of time, you are laughing right now at this statement. I was appalled. Really? How could this be happening?

We had gone from wedded bliss to another state indeed, and we needed help. But God. I have learned never to discount that God knows our hearts and hears our prayers. After months of praying and not understanding what was occurring, hairline crack by hairline crack, God placed a message on my heart that was so needed.

My husband and I loved each other for sure. We were committed to making our marriage work. But we were at odds with one another often. For ourselves, and our boys who were counting on us, we needed help. And God spoke. He unfolded a "Year of Understanding."

What if instead of trying to explain our perspectives and viewpoints to one another, and explain why the other was *wrong* in their thinking (You already know where this discussion is heading, don't you?) . . . what if we tried simply to understand? To stop and give grace. To listen to the other person's perspective. What if we truly tried to understand what each other was thinking?

Would that change our viewpoints? Would we hear how we had hurt someone, even without meaning to? Would we hear how our actions were perceived by someone, perhaps differently than what we meant to say or do? Could "understanding" change the outcome of a single event, and the next, and the next?

The year of understanding not only changed our marriage, but it changed our life as a couple, our future, and the lives of those around us. This came full circle one day when my son said to me, "Mom, you have changed. You are much more patient with me than you ever were before. And you listen to me." But God.

A pastor once said, "Change happens when we get closer to those who we are not like and see what they see, living life from their perspective." Seeing and understanding another's point of view enlightens new perspectives and brings wisdom and understanding.

- What would "A Year of Understanding" look like in your life?
- Who do you need to understand better?

- How could taking the time to understand these things change how you approach certain situations? Certain people? Or groups of people?

STEP TWO: KNOW THE CHOICE IS YOURS

We can all change our perspectives and, on some level, understand others and their thought processes, beliefs, and actions. In doing this, we will begin to gain a deeper understanding of ourselves. Our perceptions and beliefs, what we bring to every encounter, how our attitudes and behaviors were shaped, and the impacts of our views of the world.

Each of us makes judgments. These judgments are learned behaviors that are shaped from the moment we enter this world. As a baby, how we are loved, touched, and talked to matters. How those around us interact with others . . . are they kind? Do they speak with anger? Do they hate certain people, or certain kinds of people, even for no reason? Are they uplifting? Or are they critical, or demanding of their own way? Do they care about others, or do they think of themselves and their needs and desires above all else? We are a product of our environments. But even that does not define us unless we choose it to.

God gives us choices.

While we are heavily influenced by our childhood upbringing, we have a choice when it comes to how we interact with the world. We may have a propensity to be pessimistic if that is how we were raised. Or we can choose to be different. If the negativity of others impacted us poorly, we might choose that we will *not* be that way. It will take conscious effort every day, but we can change with practice, over time. The same is true of having the mindset that because my family is a certain way, I will be like them. That, too, is a choice.

I am thankful I was raised by two parents who taught me I could be *anything* I wanted to be if I worked hard enough and gave it my all. My parents went so far as saying they did not care what grades I got in school. "If you did your absolute best, then we are proud of you." Summa Cum Laude in my class later . . . I guess they were really smart parents. I had learned a valuable lesson from them—to always strive to do my best. Through this lesson, I developed a work ethic that says to never give up. I also found that "life" did not always work out. Sometimes, I failed.

Even though I gave my best, I still had a failed first marriage. I did not get the job or promotion I really wanted. I was not always successful. The truth is, sometimes bad things happen to good people, even when you are giving your best. That is a lesson I had to learn on my own. But God never leaves us. Those failed times brought successes later and brought valuable life concepts to my doorstep, such as resilience, persistence, and grit. Today, I have a wonderful husband who loves all of me and accepts every part of who I am, flaws and all. For that, I am forever grateful. I did not know that during the ten years I was alone as a single mom raising my son on my own that God was slowly molding me into the person I needed to be.

We may be a product of our environment, but we have a choice of who we are and who we are becoming. It begins with a life built through mini choices. One single choice, then another, and another—baby steps, my mom would say. Living life by trying to be understanding with others, instead of living a life of putting yourself first and attempting to be understood by others, changed my life. Living a life of seeking to understand others leads to living a life of joy found through patience, love, tolerance, wisdom, and giving grace.

STEP THREE: BRING TOLERANCE

The definition of tolerance is, "The ability or willingness to tolerate something, in particular, the existence of opinions or behavior that one does not necessarily agree with" according to Oxford Languages. *Collins English Dictionary* also defines tolerance as "the ability to bear something painful or unpleasant as in enduring a pain or hardship."

We are, by nature, judging creatures. But what if we upheld tolerance as a virtue over judgment? Simply accepting others for who they are—period. What would it look like if we were to instead of judging who someone is and trying to predict their motives to justify their actions, simply give grace and accept who they are?

The truth is, we all have one life to live, and it must be done our own way. In our world of social media, individuals are good at speaking their truths into existence and telling someone their thoughts about them. Do we ever take the time to think that our hurtful comments wound others? Do we even care that there are hearts and minds sitting in agony over our outbursts of "our truths?" We see it every day. Corporations that must do damage control because a leader has spoken out too soon. Teenagers who commit suicide because a friend has ghosted them on social media. When will we stop hurting one another and be accountable for our words and actions? "Thoughtless words cut like a sword. But the tongue of wise people brings healing" (Proverbs 12:18).

In this social climate of accepting all persons and embracing diversity, inclusion, and equity, does it not come down to living The Golden Rule, "Do unto others as you would have them do unto you." (Matthew 7:12)?

The lessons I learned from my parents long ago of treating others how we would want to be treated—being loving, kind, and accepting—seem to have become foreign concepts in today's world. Jesus said it best when he said, "Just as I have loved you, you also are to love one another" (John 13:34). The Golden Rule extends beyond loving people. It speaks to every action, word, gesture, kindness, or care extended. It speaks to giving tolerance and grace to others.

How different would our world look today if we were less full of judgment and words of hatred and anger toward even virtual strangers, and instead lived a year in understanding and embracing people unlike ourselves? What would happen if we chose to be the person who we truly aspired to be instead of making excuses of why we aren't living a life worthy of tolerance of ourselves and others? I believe the world would look very different.

The choice is ours. We can either turn from our ways or become them.

- How could you start today to be more tolerant of others?
- Instead of judging, how could you seek to understand others?
- How could your life resemble Jesus's desire to "love one another?"

Chapter 12

LIVE VICTORIOUSLY

King David, Mother Teresa, Princess Diana, Simon Sinek, Bill Gates, and countless others—what do they have in common? I do not know any of these individuals personally, nor can I speak to their successes or failures in life. The stories of their lives were not easy, I am sure. Like yours and mine, they had easy times and hard ones, successes and failures, triumphs and losses. Yet these incredible human beings, each in their own way, have made a positive impact on the lives of others and on our world by doing this one thing: They live(d) their lives authentically, as their true selves.

I am sure each of them met with adversity, challenges, rough spots, and trials along the way, but they persevered. They never lost sight of what was important in their lives and their dreams for the future. They lived to tell and speak their truths.

The truths written within this book were challenging and life-changing. They are not my truths alone. They are His. They are told to bring about one purpose: for you to live your life victoriously. To break free of the beliefs, ideas, and concepts that have confined you to live a certain kind of life. Your life is waiting. You do not have to live for anyone else or behave a certain way. All you need to be is *you*. God, and the world, are waiting for you to merely step into this truth. The life that you want is waiting for you to live out. If you will only believe in Him and trust Him.

Life contains choices. It is your choice to dream big and go after your dream life, or you can believe that you do not have a choice and your life is what has been handed to you.

As Marianne Williamson's poem, "Our Deepest Fear" says, "Your playing small does not serve the world." Be bold and courageous. Give yourself permission to shine and claim your legacy.

As with any decision, there will be costs involved, hurdles to jump, and hazards along the way. Consider this: what are the costs to living victoriously? And what is the higher price of not trying at all?

STEP ONE: EMBRACE FAILURE

By the time he died at eighty-four years of age, Thomas A. Edison had amassed a record 1,093 patents.

> *"I have not failed.*
> *I've just found 10,000 ways that won't work."*
> Thomas A. Edison

His most famous invention was the incandescent light bulb, which brought us electric light, the phonograph, and the motion picture camera. As he also stated, "Many of life's failures are people who did not realize how close they were to success when they gave up."

Failure is a part of life. But if the fear of failure keeps us from trying at all, then what is the greater loss? Failure isn't a risk; it is a certainty. You will fail. Along life's journey, things will not always go as planned. Losses will occur. Detours will happen. Yet growth and learning will occur along the way. New ideas and plans will be hatched. The price for not taking this journey at all comes at the highest cost of giving into fear. Not taking the journey ensures failure, along with the knowledge that you not only did not live up to your potential, but you also did not even try.

Consider the toddler before he begins to walk. He or she rocks back and forth on all four limbs until they try something new. They lift one arm, then one leg, and learn they can go forward. They begin to crawl. Forward momentum ensues. They next learn there is even more they can do. They are not deterred through all of the attempts and failures. They finally learn to stand. Then they again keep moving. Forward and onward, as they observe the world around them and have a desire to keep moving. They take their first step. Step, fall. Step, step, fall. They keep going. Until the time comes that they have mastered their craft, and they keep walking.

The human spirit has a driving energy to never give up and to thrive. Did you count how many times the baby failed? Do you think their mom or dad or caregiver was saying to them, "Stop; what are you thinking? Stop moving . . . you can't . . . it's too hard." Of course not.

Success is not how many times you fail. Fail, you will. What *is* important is how quickly you get back up and keep going.

STEP TWO: FORGO APPROVAL

One of the scariest and most harmful things for an individual to endure is criticism. To be laughed at, ridiculed, especially by those we love and trust. Whether it is one's parents, one's peers, or people that have earned our trust, it is difficult at any age to hear criticism and judgment. I learned this early in life growing up as a heavier kid. I remember the times of being pointed at, laughed at, and mocked. Kids learn early in life—in the beginning in elementary school—the cost to be "out there," the cost of being different from all the others. To have an idea and raise your hand comes with the uncertainty of how your answer will be received by others. You will either be labeled as "smart" or "stupid." So begins the decision to join the masses and blend in. The popular crowd, known as the "in crowd" or whatever we call cliques that have joined together, does anything to avoid standing alone. Being "out there" with the fear of being seen on our own has caused many to live mediocre lives instead of walking into their destiny. Why? Because of the fear of being criticized. Going with the "in crowd" of popular opinion is easier than living life on the edge, alone and excluded.

Unless we can reframe our thoughts on criticism and being critiqued. Original thought is how we grow as individuals, as collective humanity, and as a nation.

"Five percent of the people think;
ten percent of the people think they think,
and the other eighty-five percent
would rather die than think."
Thomas A. Edison

We cannot afford to remain stagnant or be less than who we are and who we were created to be for fear of rejection after revealing our original ideas, statements, and beliefs. There will always be people that make fun of us, push us down, or belittle our creativity or originality. These are the folks that like to be in "the pack." They find their safety in numbers and anonymity. These same people, if asked what their ideas are, often offer none. They do not have any ideas, only criticism, and they often find others to join them so they do not stand alone.

I appreciate Robert H. Schuller's famous question: "What would you attempt to do if you knew you could not fail?" It is not easy to stand alone. But the world is waiting for what you will bring. Knowing the difference that you will make by using your voice and standing on your own will be worth any possible criticism that comes. After all, God put our dreams within us. He knows everything about us—our likes, dislikes, and desires. He goes before us and is leading us to where He wants us to go if we will only trust Him.

STEP THREE: RISK IT ALL

Psalm 139:13–6 says it best: "For you formed my inward parts; you knitted me together in my mother's womb. I praise you, for I am fearfully and wonderfully made." God uses people who are willing to take risks and encounter humiliation, be ridiculed and even discredited, and look past it all to follow Him and step out in faith to the duty of what He is asking them to do. The disciples found this to be true as well. Jesus addresses this in John 15:18–25:

> If the world hates you, keep in mind that it hated me first. If you belonged to the world, it would love you as its own. As it is, you do not belong to the world, but I have chosen you out of the world. That is why the world hates you. Remember what I told you: A servant is not greater than his master. If they persecuted me, they will persecute you also.

And in John 14:27, the Bible states, "Peace I leave with you; My peace I give to you. I do not give to you as the world gives. Do not let your hearts be troubles; do not be afraid."

When we decide to serve the Lord, we step out in faith, knowing that He has us and will be with us every step of the way. My greatest position has been to be His servant. The times in my life where I am in service to Him and where He is leading, have been the times where I am completely free. Free to live out in faith what I am being called to do.

A people pleaser to the end, I often wonder if I am doing it "right." I wonder if He is happy with me. Yet

I know that He does not expect perfection, only followers who trust Him. He is the one I live for. He is my number one. I think about Jesus and what he was thinking when he heard his Father's voice from heaven saying, "This is my Son, whom I love; with him I am well pleased" (Matthew 3:17). Or thinking about King David, who was called by God as, "A man after my own heart" (1 Samuel 13:14, Acts 13:22). Like any daughter, I, too, aim to please my Father and make Him proud and happy.

Living a *victorious life* is not a half-way-done job. We cannot "kind of" reach for our full potential, like a mid-way stance that suits us part of the time—when it works to our advantage—and for the other part, we do our own thing. Being all in to serve our Lord and truly allowing Jesus to have His way with us is the only way to achieve victory. As Psalm 33:18 says, "The Lord watches over those who obey him, those who trust in his constant love."

After all, He knew you before you were born. It was Jesus that knit you together in your mother's womb. He created you to be *exactly* as you are—with your hair color, body shape, eye shape and color, talents, and more. Every part of you has been fearfully and wonderfully made. Do you believe that? Or do you still doubt Him?

Living victoriously is about living a life of intention. A life devoted to being His servant, to follow His leading wherever that leads you. Being His involves accepting yourself and loving yourself for all of you, exactly as you are. It has been said, "God does not call the equipped, He equips the called." I am thankful for the countless examples He has given us in the Bible that speak to this. David and Goliath, for example—a little shepherd boy who slew a giant and became a king. David, who was not perfect by any stretch of the imagination. Like you and me, he was a flawed human being who was also called, "a man after God's own heart." This is the same David, who shares the same lineage that brought us Jesus, our Savior of the World.

Isaiah 61:2–3 says, "To proclaim the year of the Lord's favor and the day of vengeance of our God, to comfort all who mourn, and provide for those who grieve in Zion. To bestow on them a crown of beauty instead of ashes." This beautiful passage is a symbol of hope. It goes on to say, "The oil of joy instead of mourning, and a garment of praise instead of a spirit of despair. They will be called oaks of righteousness, a planting of the Lord for the display of his splendor." God is painting a picture that shows who wins in the end. That no matter what we go through, no matter our heartbreak and pain, He will use it all. He beckons us to trust and obey Him, and He will display His glory.

Indeed, we'll receive a crown of beauty instead of ashes. Jesus wastes nothing. Every event that we have gone through in our lives has not been by accident. They are not coincidences. We can choose to allow God to use our stories for His glory through His molding us into the people He created us to be. Our victorious lives await us. Have confidence that the Lord who brought Israel out of Egypt, who parted the Red Sea, who performed miracles yesterday, is still alive and well and is working through you and me if we allow it. Stand in the fullness of your true potential by risking it all. "Take up your cross and follow me," He says in Matthew 16:24.

The choice is yours. Remember, baby steps.

Jesus said in Matthew 16:26, "For whoever would save his life will lose it, but whoever loses his life for my sake will find it."

- What is keeping you from following Jesus and saying, "I trust you. Your will be done."
- What does it look like to live in the trueness of who you were created to be?
- Do you fear giving up control of your life to God?
- What is holding you back from giving Him your all and becoming His disciple?

STEP FOUR: BE BRILLIANT

When we accept ourselves in the fullest manner, we are able to share ourselves with others and truly impact lives.

What would it feel like to risk it all? As a self-professed person who desires control in every aspect of my life, the hardest thing has been to realize that I have very little control of my life. Life can completely change in an instant. I know. In an instant, happily ever after can end, without a moment's notice. In an instant, the car from behind can hit you leaving you spinning then waking up to find your life has been permanently altered. In an instant, your mind can become a foreign place and the world around you unknown.

Only God knows what is before me in my future. The mountain tops on which I'll stand and the valleys that He will carry me through. Life is precious. In a moment, it is perfect, and the next it could be tragic.

As a former control freak, I have truly learned to let go and let God. Jesus is our constant. He is the same yesterday, today, and tomorrow. I have learned through the difficult lessons of my life that truly, God knows best. He knows me at my innermost being. He knows what I think before I can even utter a word or form a thought in my mind (Psalms 139:13). My Savior knows me inside and out. Even though, at one time, I doubted if He really did know. What I felt was too much for me to handle, yet He taught me I am stronger than I think. It was at this lowest point, this most painful time in my life, that He taught me: When I am weak, He is strong. He taught me to simply let go. His grace is enough, and He will carry me through when I am too frail and tired for one more step.

I think it is because of this absolute trust and assurance that I have experienced in our Lord, that I'm able to say, "I trust you, Lord." When I can't see a way forward through the dark or the fog, I know He can. He sees the path ahead and says He has me. When I don't know how I am going to survive a situation, He shows me that He cares and holds my hand through it.

Through this, I have learned to accept Him and His love for me . . . and to finally love myself fully—every part of me. Like you, I am flawed. While I am strong and confident, knowledgeable, and powerful, I am also weak and scared, unknowing, and delicate. I make mistakes and He loves me through it all.

Through this acknowledgment of the wholeness of me, I have stepped into my full acceptance of "me" and the ability to fully love and embrace others for who they are.

STEP FIVE: TRUST

"Trust in the Lord with all your heart and lean not on your own understanding; in all your ways submit to him, and he will make your paths straight" (Proverbs 3:5–6). A life dedicated to the Lord is not easy. It does not come without challenges and trials. I used to think that I had seen it all. That I had been through so much in life, nothing could surprise me. I have been wrong. Just when I think I have been stretched far enough, Jesus lets me know I can stretch a little more. Whether this has been through situations and events or through learning different perspectives from people that are different from me, what I have learned is that Jesus came for everyone. He came to love and accept everyone into His kingdom. He did not come to make exceptions or to say, "Everyone but you *and your kind.*"

My heart has grieved from the judgment others inflict on people they do not know, who they do not even try to understand. People that are different from them. I have learned the urgency of His pleadings with all of us to love. Love is kind. Love is patient. Love is not loving only those that look like us, think like us, or behave like us. No, that is not love. Love loves all.

Silent No More. As He inspired the contents of this book, it is no accident that this chapter, too, evolved into being. Twelve in biblical perspective means perfection. As I hear the words of my soul speaking, this book would not be complete without a plea for understanding, this twelfth chapter. I have had my heart stretched to understand beyond what I ever could have imagined. To truly venture into and explore an unknown. Truly love does conquer all. Through understanding, I have experienced an all-out love that exceeds even my wildest dreams and has brought more joy than I ever thought was possible. It has surprised me and touched me in ways that I cannot even describe. I have learned this love through understanding what I did not know and learning through someone else's eyes. We can only do this, though, through Jesus living in us and allowing us to see others as He sees us. Unique and beautiful.

As we stand today, our nation is facing one of the hardest times. Between the hatred and discrimination across all kinds of lines and people: Black, white, Asian, Jew, gay, straight, bi, trans, thin, fat, rich, and poor. You name it, wherever you stand on the issues or these people, there is someone in complete opposition to where you believe, and we are tearing each other and our world apart through it.

My mom once told me, "Love knows no bounds." From a woman that even from her grave is telling the world to love one another, like most moms, she is right. Love is our only answer.

This book began as a whole different idea from where we sit now. God works like that. He knew what He intended. And as I submitted to Him every time my fingers touched the page, He had His way through me to the words I know He inspired. The title has remained as is, and His truth, and mine as His servant, have been revealed.

We are living in an age where we can no longer afford to be silent. We must stand up and act through love and grace toward everyone. Hatred knows no bounds and will destroy us. We must look to God, who is the only answer for the multitude of problems our world faces. As we put our trust in Him and Him alone, as it says in John 8:32, "Then you will know the truth, and the truth will set you free."

My people matter.

For His Glory. Amen.

ABOUT THE AUTHOR

As a life-long follower of Christ, Jody L. Dedon has devoted her life to learning and deepening her faith while sharing her love for the Lord with others. Since early childhood, she has felt a special connection and calling from the Lord. Her faith has grown through the trials of life, which have stretched and molded her into the person she is today. Through this lens, Jody has learned to, above all, seek His will and look for His presence as "wisdom is revealed over time and through circumstances."

Raised by parents who were committed to community service, Jody believes strongly in servant leadership and the power of one to make a difference. Her personal mission is to make a positive difference in the lives of others. She enjoys opportunities to bring her infectious energy and zeal for life to empower individuals to see the beauty inside of them and unlock their true potential. Jody describes herself as a "work in progress."

Jody has served the Indianapolis community in various roles throughout her career. Jody has led notable non-profit organizations as executive director and director of development. Today, Jody holds a senior leadership position managing business development and marketing for a major engineering firm in Indianapolis, Indiana.

A lover of family and traditions, Jody and her husband, Craig, live in Indianapolis with their four sons and two dogs.